Cambridge Elements

Elements on Women in the History of Philosophy
edited by
Jacqueline Broad
Monash University

PLATONIST WOMEN

Crystal Addey
University College Cork

Shaftesbury Road, Cambridge CB2 8EA, United Kingdom

One Liberty Plaza, 20th Floor, New York, NY 10006, USA

477 Williamstown Road, Port Melbourne, VIC 3207, Australia

314–321, 3rd Floor, Plot 3, Splendor Forum, Jasola District Centre, New Delhi – 110025, India

103 Penang Road, #05–06/07, Visioncrest Commercial, Singapore 238467

Cambridge University Press is part of Cambridge University Press & Assessment, a department of the University of Cambridge.

We share the University's mission to contribute to society through the pursuit of education, learning and research at the highest international levels of excellence.

www.cambridge.org
Information on this title: www.cambridge.org/9781009538855

DOI: 10.1017/9781009158893

© Crystal Addey 2025

This publication is in copyright. Subject to statutory exception and to the provisions of relevant collective licensing agreements, no reproduction of any part may take place without the written permission of Cambridge University Press & Assessment.

When citing this work, please include a reference to the DOI 10.1017/9781009158893

First published 2025

A catalogue record for this publication is available from the British Library

ISBN 978-1-009-53885-5 Hardback
ISBN 978-1-009-15890-9 Paperback
ISSN 2634-4645 (online)
ISSN 2634-4637 (print)

Cambridge University Press & Assessment has no responsibility for the persistence or accuracy of URLs for external or third-party internet websites referred to in this publication and does not guarantee that any content on such websites is, or will remain, accurate or appropriate.

For EU product safety concerns, contact us at Calle de José Abascal, 56, 1°, 28003 Madrid, Spain, or email eugpsr@cambridge.org

Platonist Women

Elements on Women in the History of Philosophy

DOI: 10.1017/9781009158893
First published online: August 2025

Crystal Addey
University College Cork
Author for correspondence: Crystal Addey, crystal.addey@ucc.ie

Abstract: This Element examines the roles and activities of women and their contributions to the Platonic tradition from Plato's time – fifth and fourth centuries BCE – through to the sixth century CE. Drawing on recent research on female agency, gender studies, and the connections between ancient philosophy and religious traditions, this Element re-assesses the multifaceted roles of women within Platonism. Methodologically, any assessment of ancient women philosophers must consider the contexts of the production, transmission and (partial) survival of the range of evidence attesting to their activities, and the historical minimisation or elision of women's intellectual contributions within the western philosophical tradition, science and the academy. As such, this Element argues that the existing evidence allows us to glimpse a much wider pattern of female philosophical and intellectual activity within the Platonic tradition and that we should be careful not to underestimate or minimise the significance of ancient women within the history of Platonism.

Keywords: Platonist women, Middle Platonist women, Neoplatonist women, female philosophers, philosopher-priestesses

© Crystal Addey 2025

ISBNs: 9781009538855 (HB), 9781009158909 (PB), 9781009158893 (OC)
ISSNs: 2634-4645 (online), 2634-4637 (print)

Contents

1 Introduction: Catching a Glimpse of a World of Women   1

2 Women in the World of Plato   15

3 Women in Later Platonism   35

4 Female Philosophers and Philosophical Writing   48

5 Platonic Philosopher-Priestesses   60

6 Conclusion: The Significance of Platonist Women   75

   List of Abbreviations   77

   References   78

1 Introduction: Catching a Glimpse of a World of Women

Contemporary readers of Plato may be familiar with Diotima of Mantinea and Aspasia of Miletus, who feature indirectly in Plato's *Symposium* and *Menexenus* respectively, as well as with Plato's views of women expressed throughout the dialogues (especially those in the *Republic*). However, it is not so well-known that many women engaged with Plato's philosophy both during his lifetime and in subsequent periods of antiquity – as readers of his works, students, teachers, patrons, members and supporters of philosophical schools and communities, ethical role models, and as philosophers in their own right. Women were actively involved in the Platonic tradition from the time of Plato (ca. 429–347 BCE) through to the sixth century CE, over the course of almost a millennium.

For the purposes of this Element, three chronological phases of the Platonic tradition are crucial: first, we begin with Plato and his philosophical school, the Academy, established in 387 BCE in classical Athens, and his successor, Speusippus (who succeeded the Headship when Plato died in 347 BCE). The longevity of the Academy is contested but the consensus is that it ceased to operate in the grounds of the Academy in 86 BCE.[1]

The next phase of the Platonic tradition is referred to as 'Middle Platonism', a modern term denoting Platonist philosophers and their theories in the late Hellenistic and Roman periods (approximately 88 BCE to 220 CE); the term refers to the chronological period rather than implying a coherent or doctrinally unified movement (Dillon 1996: 422–423). Since evidence for women engaging with Plato's philosophy within the context of Middle Platonism comes from the works of Plutarch of Chaeronea (ca.45/46–120 CE), this Element will focus particularly on Plutarch's era, the first and second centuries CE. Finally, in late antiquity (approximately the third to eighth centuries CE) we see the development of 'Neoplatonism', a modern designation invented by German philologists who saw this movement as inherently different from and inferior to Plato's philosophy (Addey 2014a: 1 n.2). Plotinus (205–270 CE) is usually seen as the founder of Neoplatonism. Yet it has been noted that Plotinus and many of his philosophic successors would have been surprised at the suggestion that he was founding something new, since many saw Plotinus as working in the same tradition as Numenius (a philosopher usually described as 'Middle Platonist' or 'Neopythagorean'). Furthermore, Plotinus drew on the philosophy of his teacher, Ammonius Saccas, a somewhat obscure figure (Tarrant *et al.* 2017: 5). In fact, Plotinus and his 'Neoplatonist' successors – as well as earlier 'Middle Platonists' – would have identified themselves simply as 'Platonists'.

---

[1] See Bonazzi 2020: 242–255; Tarrant *et al.* 2017: 4–5; Kalligas *et al.* 2020: 1, 6. On Plato's successors in the Old Academy, see Dillon 2003.

Therefore, these modern classifications are problematic, since they obscure the strong continuity linking Middle Platonism and Neoplatonism (O'Meara 2003: 3 n.1). These terms are used in this Element only as chronological designations, without the pejorative associations originally attached to the term 'Neoplatonism'.

'Platonist women' refers to the women who feature in Plato's dialogues or who were members of the Academy (during Plato's lifetime and subsequently) in classical Athens. These women were not from Athens: they are presented as being from other city-states (*poleis*) in Greece and Asia Minor. The term 'Platonist women', as used in this work, also refers to the women associated with Middle Platonism and Neoplatonism. Middle Platonist women were linked with Delphi, as well as with Plutarch's home-town, Chaeronea in Boeotia, but lived during the Roman imperial period when Greece was ruled by Rome (Roskam 2021: 1–2). Neoplatonist women hail from various regions across the Mediterranean and were associated with Neoplatonic philosophical schools: Plotinus' school in Rome, Iamblichus' school in Apamea, Syria, Aedesius' and Sosipatra's school in Pergamon, Asia Minor, and the Athenian and Alexandrian Neoplatonic Schools.[2] The women associated with Plotinus' school at Rome (and with Porphyry) are something of an outlier geographically, in the sense that most of these women were from the Greek East (the Eastern half of the Roman Empire) or Egypt. While we have little knowledge of their socio-economic status, it can be assumed that the vast majority (though perhaps not all) of these women were from aristocratic families. This was certainly the case with most ancient male philosophers (though there were important exceptions), since one had to have the 'leisure time' to study philosophy and the financial resources to travel to – and support oneself while at – various philosophical schools.

This Element examines the roles and activities of Platonist women and their contributions to Platonism, from the fifth century BCE (relating to the dramatic dates of Plato's dialogues featuring women) through to 529 CE, when the Athenian School of Neoplatonism was closed by Emperor Justinian. Drawing on recent research on female agency, gender studies, and the inextricable connections between ancient philosophy and religious traditions, this Element will re-assess the epistemic agency of women within the Platonic tradition. It evidences that these women were philosophers in their own right, heads, supporters and patrons of philosophical schools, teachers, students, empowering role models (especially in relation to ethics and the cultivation of the virtues), significant catalysts for philosophical ideas and writings, and, at least in some cases, authors of philosophical works.

---

[2] On the location of Iamblichus' School, see Balty 1988: 95.

Other Elements in this series – Women in the History of Philosophy, especially Caterina Pellò's *Pythagorean Women* and Dawn LaValle Norman's *Early Christian Women* – cover women living in the same centuries as those assessed here. Pythagorean philosophy and communities were an important inspiration for Plato and for Neoplatonists such as Iamblichus, especially with regard to the important roles of women within philosophical practice and communities. Early Christian women who are presented as philosophers, such as Macrina, lived around the same time as the Neoplatonist philosopher, Sosipatra, and earlier than Neoplatonists such as Hypatia of Alexandria and Asclepigeneia of Athens. In both cases, there are often considerable overlap in the depictions and motifs surrounding these philosophical women. The focus in this Element on Platonist women is not meant to suggest that they belong to a separate genealogy from women associated with Pythagoreanism or early Christianity; rather, these connections are acknowledged.

Complex methodological problems surround any attempt to assess the philosophical contributions of women within the Platonic tradition and within ancient philosophy in a broader sense. It is vital to examine these issues since they have important implications for any interpretation of these ancient women.

1.1 What Is (Ancient) 'Philosophy' and Who Counts as a 'Philosopher'?

Many women were associated with Plato and the Academy, and with Middle Platonist and Neoplatonist philosophers and philosophical schools. Most (although not all) of them were the female relatives – the mothers, wives or daughters – of male philosophers. How do we ascertain whether they can be categorised as 'philosophers', especially if they are not explicitly identified as such? This methodological difficulty relates to how we classify female philosophers and their activities, which itself is based on how we define 'philosophy' and 'philosophical activity'.[3]

When we envisage a philosopher in the contemporary world, we might think of a professional who writes philosophical works and perhaps teaches and delivers lectures. Philosophy in antiquity was also sometimes a profession: some philosophers held public paid chairs, and many were active and respected members of their communities. However, philosophical schools frequently had a patron (Dillon 2004: 418). Philosophy in antiquity often presupposed a good level of education (*paideia*) and literacy on the part of the aspiring philosopher. Women's access to education varied 'from. . . . place to place, through time, and in relation to social classses, and individual households' (Deslauriers 2012:

---

[3] See O'Reilly & Pellô 2023: 11–13.

352). Yet some women (especially aristocratic) had access to education, even if this was sporadic and informal, and were literate and even bilingual. However, ancient philosophers did not necessarily always write philosophical works: philosophy in antiquity was as much an oral practice as a written one (Deslauriers 2012: 344). Socrates, who features in Plato's works and is often taken to represent Plato's philosopher par excellence, wrote nothing. The accounts we have of his philosophical ideas come from the works of Plato and Socratic writers (Ahbel-Rappe 2009: 6–7). Plato's Academy held spoken discourse as the primary means of philosophical investigation. Philosophy was commonly practised in public contexts and spaces, as is often depicted in Plato's dialogues. Consequently, the restrictions on public speech imposed upon women must be considered alongside this preferred mode of philosophical activity (Deslauriers 2012: 344). Ancient philosophers also delivered public lectures (open to all), while some Neoplatonists acted as political advisors to local officials, attending therein public meetings on city affairs.[4] Partially because philosophical activity often took place in public contexts and frequently involved teaching or studying in public, it is often said that philosophy was implicitly coded as a male or masculine practice in Graeco-Roman antiquity which women were excluded from. After all, aristocratic women in classical Athens were largely prohibited from public roles (with the important exception of the role of priestess, discussed in Section 1.1.2) and social restrictions entailed that they could not move around freely in public spaces without a male relative or guardian, or socialise with men who were not relatives. Marguerite Deslauriers (2012: 345) exemplifies this view: 'Philosophy, then, was a social practice, engagement with which was predicated on education and on certain social freedoms, neither of which women enjoyed.' Following Dawn LaValle Norman (2022: 5), I would like to challenge this view by suggesting that women were involved in social philosophical life in antiquity – particularly because philosophy was considered to be a way of life and, as such, was often practised in domestic, small-scale and private contexts. Additionally, it seems sensible to adhere to simple definitions of 'philosophy' and 'philosophical activity', which reflect ancient – especially Platonic – views of their nature. Put otherwise, internal definitions of 'philosophy' in antiquity must be employed so as to avoid anachronism (Addey 2022: 12). In this regard, Gillian Clark and Tessa Rajak (2002: 1) have defined philosophy as 'literally, the love of wisdom, the need to understand what the world is like and how human beings should live'. Jonathan Barnes expands on this definition in

---

[4] On Plato's public lecture entitled 'On the Good', see the testimonies in Riginos 1976: 124–127. On Plotinus' public lectures, see Porphyry, *Plot.* 13; Dillon 2004: 405. For Proclus' involvement in public affairs, see Marinus, *Proc.* 15; Dillon 2004: 415.

relation to categorising the 'philosopher': ' ... to call oneself, or be called, *philosophos* is to declare a love of wisdom, a readiness to study things human and divine' (Barnes 2002: 293). Conceptualising philosophy in this broader sense facilitates a more inclusive approach towards women's participation in ancient philosophical practice.

1.1.1 Philosophy as a Way of Life and Domestic Contexts

Although ancient philosophy was a social practice often linked with public contexts, there are several ways in which philosophy had a much broader scope in the ancient world which facilitated women's access: (1) the small-scale and often domestic, or semi-domestic, contexts and locations of most ancient philosophical schools and of philosophical practice; (2) the fact that philosophy was considered a 'way of life' – rather than merely a profession, discursive activity, or intellectual discipline – in antiquity; and (3) the close connections between ancient philosophy and religion.

Ancient philosophical schools were often small-scale and located in domestic or semi-domestic contexts, such as the household of a patron.[5] John Dillon notes:

> One of the first things we have to do ... when approaching the study of ancient centres of learning, whether philosophical, medical, legal or rhetorical, is to think small. Even the model of the mediaeval university presents us with something far too elaborate. (Dillon 2004: 402)

Even in the case of the Academy, where teaching frequently took place in public areas such as the gymnasium, Plato also taught students in the garden of his home on the Academy's grounds.[6] When we move to Middle Platonism and Neoplatonism we find philosophical schools located in the household of a philosopher or patron, such as Plotinus' school in Rome which was established in the household of one of his students, Gemina the Elder (Porphyry, *Plot.* 9.1-2; see Section 3). In addition to the physical scale and location of philosophical schools, we know that philosophy was practised informally in domestic contexts from Middle Platonism onwards: for example, many philosophers, like Plutarch and Porphyry, discussed and practised philosophy with their female family members (Clark 2007: 153–172). These domestic contexts were just as important for the Platonic tradition as the public aspects of philosophical activity and facilitated the inclusion of women within philosophical practices and schools.

---

[5] On philosophical practice within domestic contexts in late antiquity, see Clark 2007: 153–172.
[6] D.L. 3.5. See Baltes 1993: 7.

Moreover, since philosophy was conceived as 'a way of life', a view shared by most of the classical, Hellenistic and Roman philosophical schools, the practice was envisaged as far more than merely an intellectual pursuit or profession in antiquity – rather, it was 'a method of spiritual progress which demanded a radical . . . transformation of the individual's way of being' (Hadot 1995: 265, 2002: 3–4, 23, 91–171). As such, philosophy, in its exercise and effort to achieve wisdom and in its goal – wisdom, was an embodied practice embedded in daily life. The ancient philosophical school represents 'a form of life defined by an ideal of wisdom' (Hadot 1995: 59). For the ancients, the word *philo-sophia* – the 'love of wisdom' – was enough to express this conception of philosophy (Hadot 1995: 265). In the *Symposium*, Plato's Socrates – while relating the teaching of the philosopher-priestess Diotima – shows how the philosopher could be identified with the mythological spirit of Eros, who lacked wisdom but knew how to acquire it (*Symp.* 204b3-5). For later traditions such as Stoicism, wisdom and, correspondingly philosophy, was that which brought peace of mind (*ataraxia*) and inner freedom/self-sufficiency (*autarkeia*) and, in some traditions like Neoplatonism, a cosmic consciousness (Hadot 1995: 265). In Platonic terms, it was considered that the effort to attain – and attainment of – wisdom would transform the life and soul of the philosopher and affect his or her daily life profoundly. Therefore, Platonic philosophers aimed to live their everyday lives in accordance with the 'norm of wisdom'. This conception centralises the Socratic focus on ethics, moral conduct, and the importance of examining what makes a good life, although it extends well beyond this. It is vital to note that the traditional tripartition of (ancient) philosophy into physics, ethics and logic refers to the parts of *philosophical discourse*, rather than to *philosophy* itself (Hadot 1995: 267).

Philosophy was seen as a therapeutic 'mode of existing-in-the world' which had to be practised continually (Hadot 1995: 264–266). For Plato and later Platonist philosophers, philosophy primarily consisted of the 'care of the soul' (*Phd.* 64e4-7) through the investigation of reality and the cultivation and development of the virtues (or excellences) in order to lead a good life (*Resp.* VII, 518d-e); this 'care of the soul' was considered to involve care of the souls of others as well.[7] Overall, this conception of philosophy as a daily practice which was a continuous, lifelong endeavour practised in every sphere of life allows for the consideration of a much wider range of female philosophical activity.

---

[7] Although a controversial issue, Plato portrays Socrates – his philosopher par excellence – as showing great care for his philosophic interlocutors and companions: see Hadot 2002: 36–38 and the essays collected in Diduch & Harding 2018. In the Myth of the Cave, Plato indicates that the philosopher must return to the cave, to the world, even after ascending to the intelligible world and 'seeing' the Form of the Good, in order to try to help others: *Resp.* VII, 516e, 519e-520b.

1.1.2 Philosophy and Religion in the Platonic Tradition

The conception of philosophy as a way of life underlies the close connections between religion and philosophy for Plato and later Platonists, since philosophy was seen as the investigation of reality in all its aspects (divine, more-than-human and human, metaphysical, cosmic, ethical and epistemological) and as a 'care for the soul' in relation to the parameters of reality. Plato's approach towards religion is much contested. Until recently, scholars of ancient philosophy have shown a remarkable reluctance in seeing religion as a significant or intrinsic aspect of his philosophy, and, as such, have largely ignored the theological and religious elements in his writings. However, recent scholarship has begun to explore the religious dimensions of Plato's thought. For example, Andrea Nightingale argues that religion was extremely important for Plato's philosophy:

> Plato ... did not think that humans keep the universe alone. In his middle-period dialogues, the gods played important roles in human life and the afterlife. These gods had perfect reason, and they judged human lives with complete justice. In the late dialogues *Timaeus* and *Laws*, gods took on an even greater role: they moved the heavens and governed the entire cosmos. Philosophers could see the 'visible gods' in the bodies of the star-gods. Plato also gave the soul divine capacities: living in a human body on earth, it could actualize its divinity by practicing philosophy. Finally, Plato identified the Forms as divine. When the philosopher contemplated the Forms, then, each with its own essence, he also encountered divinity ... Plato depicts the philosopher as seeing a divine epiphany when he contemplates the Forms. (Nightingale 2021: 3–4)

Additionally, Plato's Socrates defines the goal of philosophy as ' ... to become like a god insofar as this is possible' (Plato, *Tht.* 176b: ὁμοίωσις θεῷ κατὰ τὸ δυνατόν). Yet despite this, most scholars tend to overlook Plato's references to Greek religious practices because they fall outside of the contemporary philosophical purview (Nightingale 2021: 7). The latter implicitly draws on the modern Enlightenment opposition between reason and religion, but the ancient Greeks did not conceive of philosophy as opposed to religion in this way.[8]

Plato's depiction of the religiosity of both Socrates and Diotima further suggests that he saw religion as extremely important – maybe even essential and intrinsic – for the practising philosopher. Plato presents Socrates'

---

[8] On the mutually inclusive relationship between reason and ritual in Neoplatonism and the post-Enlightenment assumptions often applied to ancient ritual and religious practices, see Addey 2014a: 171–213.

philosophical mission and lifestyle as catalysed by a Delphic oracular response received by Socrates' friend Chaerephon: when the latter inquired if anyone was wiser than Socrates, the Pythia's oracle replied that there was no one wiser (Plato, *Ap.* 21a3-7). So, in an effort to understand the meaning of this oracle, Socrates began his investigation into its meaning by an elenctic questioning of those with a reputation for expertise and wisdom in their respective fields (*Ap.* 21b-22e). For Socrates, this was his service to Apollo undertaken at the god's behest; indeed, he claims that his ongoing philosophical investigations stem from this initial inquiry (*Ap.* 22a4, 23b4-c1, 33c5-9). Across multiple works, Plato also frequently has Socrates discuss his *daimonion* – his divine 'voice' or 'sign' – which warned him from doing something in error.[9] This was his 'customary mode of divination' (*Ap.* 40a4: ἡ γὰρ εἰωθυῖά μοι μαντικὴ) and Socrates elsewhere describes himself or the soul as a seer (*mantis*) in both the *Phaedo* (85b4-6) and *Phaedrus* (242c5-7). Moreover, Plato places one of his most powerful speeches in the mouth of a priestess, Diotima, and has her claim that philosophy is a divine or, more accurately, a daimonic activity (as explored in Sections 2.1.1 and 5.1).

For later Platonist philosophers, the connections between religion and philosophy were even more overt. The Middle Platonist Plutarch of Chaeronea was priest at the Delphic Oracle of Apollo for twenty five or thirty years. Porphyry frequently writes about religious traditions and myth in a wide range of his philosophical works. Later Neoplatonist philosophers developed the concept of 'theurgy' – a set of ritual practices coupled with philosophical inquiry and the cultivation of the virtues – which they considered necessary for the ascent of the human soul to the intelligible world of the gods and for the manifestation of the divine in embodied, human life (Addey 2014a). These aspects of Plato's philosophy and Platonism are often downplayed by contemporary scholars, but if we elide these religious aspects of Platonism, we miss a central aspect of the philosophy of Plato and later Platonist philosophers and – most significantly for our purposes here – a crucial dimension of the roles of Platonist women.

The close connections between religion and philosophy had significant implications for ancient women philosophers. The one public role that most women could hold in Graeco-Roman antiquity – from archaic Greece right through to late antiquity – was that of priestess. As Joan Breton Connelly emphasises, ' … religious office presented the one arena where women assumed roles equal and comparable to those of men' (Connelly 2007: 2). Starting with Plato's presentation of Diotima as a priestess in the *Symposium*,

---

[9] Socrates' *daimonion* as a divine 'voice': *Phaedr.* 242c2, *Ap.* 31d4; as a divine 'sign': *Euthyd.*, 272e5; *Resp.* VI, 496c4; *Phaedr.* 242c1; *Ap.* 40b1-2, 40c3, 41d7. For a review of scholarship on the *daimonion* of Socrates in Plato and its reception in Neoplatonism, see Addey 2014b: 51–72.

many women associated with the Platonic tradition were presented as philosopher-priestesses and some historical women associated with later Platonism were priestesses or priestess-like figures, who combined ritual expertise with philosophical practice (see Section 5).

1.2 Source Problems

When examining Platonist women, there are complex methodological issues relating to our sources. First, almost no philosophical works authored by female Platonist philosophers survive. This lack of writings by women means that we do not hear their ideas, arguments, theories or even their voices directly. It is often assumed that most women in this tradition did not write philosophical works, yet we do have some evidence for several Platonist women's writings, even if these works were not necessarily preserved or transmitted in later periods (see Section 4). Overall, the evidence that survives is authored by male, aristocratic writers. As such, many women associated with the Platonic tradition are only mentioned in one (male-authored) source, as is the case with Diotima, Sosipatra and Asclepigeneia. It is worth reflecting that had the works they feature in not survived, we would not even know of the existence of these women.

The textual sources of evidence that attest to women's involvement in the Platonic tradition tend to fall into three genres, each of which had their own specific conventions and stylistic features:

(1) Philosophical dialogue: women's speeches are reported by male philosophers (as in Plato's works) or women feature directly as interlocutors but do not speak for themselves (as in Plutarch's works). Even though both Plato's and Plutarch's dialogues tend to base their interlocutors on historical figures known to them personally or by reputation, it is notoriously difficult to disentangle the fictional and possibly historical elements in their depictions.
(2) Philosophical letters: women are sometimes the recipients of philosophical letters authored by male philosophers and may have been the latter's correspondents. This is despite the fact that the letters presumably written by women to male philosophers do not survive and were probably not preserved even in antiquity.
(3) Late antique *Lives*: women associated with Plato, Middle Platonism and Neoplatonism are often mentioned or examined in late antique *Lives,* which are a kind of 'biographical account' of ancient philosophers. These sources offer idealised and hagiographical portraits of their biographical subjects,

including symbolic gestures, in the form of anecdotes and evocative images, meant to reveal the character or quality of the philosopher rather than give a historical or chronological account of his or her entire life.[10]

With each type of genre, we need to pay close attention to the way that the conventions of the philosophical or literary genre affect the portrayal of the women therein (LaValle Norman 2022).

In relation to the recent post-structuralist 'literary turn', Elizabeth Clark (1998: 18) has argued against reading Late antique *Lives* as '... mines for the construction of social history'. Her critique challenges *any* historical interpretation of late antique biographies but focuses especially on the *Lives* which offer portraits of women (Clark 1998: 1–31). She claims that these *Lives* share many features with the genre of the ancient novel rather than with classical biographies of public figures.[11] Her analysis focuses on Gregory of Nyssa's Macrina, but her arguments have implications for any interpretation of the women depicted in the *Lives*.[12] She notes that Gregory's presentation of Macrina draws on Plato's portrayal of Diotima and uses David Halperin's influential study which argued that Plato invented Diotima in order to appropriate qualities considered as 'feminine' (Halperin 1990). Similarly, Clark argues that the *Lives* present their heroines as teachers of wisdom as a literary trope with the same appropriative aim (Clark 1998: 21–27). In her analysis, Gregory puppets the voice of Macrina to think through troubling theological and intellectual issues and as a shaming device for his Christian male readers (Clark 1998: 26–30). In this interpretation, the women portrayed in the *Lives* do not reflect or represent 'real' historical women but relate to the literary or theological 'functions' of the text.

Several factors mitigate against such stark readings of portrayals of ancient women. First, another crucial source of evidence used in this Element is epigraphic – that is, inscriptions, which can provide an important corrective to such interpretations. Historical women *are* attested explicitly as 'philosophers' in inscriptions from the Roman imperial period onwards; in at least a few cases, inscriptions name Platonist women, explicitly confirming their historicity.[13] Furthermore, although close attention needs to be paid to the rhetorical and literary strategies used by ancient male biographers to characterise their subjects, interpreting ancient portrayals of women *solely* in relation to these

---
[10] See the classic study of late antique biography: Cox 1983: xi–xvi.
[11] Clark 1998: 16–17; Cooper 1996: 1–44.
[12] For analysis of these methodological issues in relation to early Christian women, see Dawn LaValle Norman's Element in this series.
[13] On inscriptions commemorating women as 'philosophers' in the Roman imperial period, see Barnes 2002: 293–306; Addey 2022: 18–22.

functions has the potential to minimise or even entirely elide women's epistemic agency. After all, the only epistemic agent to emerge intact from post-structuralist readings is the ancient male biographer. As such, post-structuralist approaches may contribute to the reification or reinforcement of patriarchal structures that elide or marginalise women's intellectual activities and contributions.

Virginia Burrus strategically attempts to get behind male-authored texts portraying women to 'historical' women by arguing that 'the discursive space occupied by Plato's Diotima or Gregory's Macrina might also correlate, however inexactly, with the social roles and influence of women' and that the representation of women in male-centred texts 'may stand in for (without exactly reproducing) the intrusive presence of women in the always incomplete formation of male homosocial communities' (Burrus 2005: 259). Anna Christensen has recently argued convincingly that Gregory's presentation of Macrina's philosophical arguments and way of life are informative of her philosophical activity (Christensen 2023: 170–189).

Even if biographical depictions of women are fictitious (or fictionalised), they influenced subsequent generations of ancient women.[14] For example, Diotima – in her role as a prototype philosopher-priestess – seems to have influenced later, historical female philosophers in their roles of ritual experts and priestesses (see Section 5).Therefore, 'the turn to "reception studies" is one way of getting beyond the difficult relationship between literary portrayals of female roles and the historical reality of women' (LaValle Norman 2022: 6). Even Elizabeth Clark admits that there are 'traces' of Macrina that remain (1998: 31). While paying attention to the 'functions' women play in literary texts, it is important to exercise caution in interpreting the depictions of women in these *Lives* solely in this way, given that this hermeneutic strategy effectively elides the agency and roles of women in antiquity, thus reifying patriarchal strategies and ideas about women that still exist today. After all, there has been little post-structuralist criticism of using late antique *Lives* to supply (historical) biographical information about male philosophers. Ancient male authors were presenting women within the realm of what was considered possible for women in terms of social roles and influence, and their accounts reveal traces of women's historical lives.

In the three types of textual sources, we mostly hear about the interaction of these women with male philosophers, as their teachers, students, colleagues or family members. For example, women philosophers tend to be mentioned in passing in late antique *Lives*, in relation to their role as a teacher, student or

---

[14] See LaValle Norman 2022: 6, on the ways in which biographical accounts 'both reflect and enact change', using the example of the influence of Thecla on Macrina and her mother.

relative of a male philosopher who is the main subject of the work. We rarely, if ever, hear about women's interactions with each other, possibly because male philosophers were uninterested or did not necessarily have access to female-to-female conversations and intellectual activities, factors which often related to the marginalisation of groups treated as subordinate, including women. Suzanne Dixon has observed a similar pattern in her study of Roman women: elite men might have been only partially aware of the actions of women, children and slaves, unless these actions infringed upon them. The exclusions of our surviving sources owe something to the unconscious marginalisation of the subordinate groups involved (Dixon 2001: 21). Nevertheless, there are faint trances of female-to-female philosophical transmission in our sources, which will be explored in this Element.

1.3 Women as Epistemic Agents: Moving beyond Silence and Marginalisation

When assessing the intellectual endeavours of ancient women, it is vital to take into account the long-term historical minimisation or elision of women's intellectual activities and contributions within the western philosophical tradition, science and the academy.[15] Sara Brill and Catherine McKeen note that several timeframes are important when examining ancient women philosophers: we must consider whether women were treated as epistemic agents in their own time. It is also vital to examine whether women were treated as thinkers and knowers in the tradition of textual transmission, examining the ways in which past and contemporary receptions of ancient texts are influenced by past and contemporary gender conditions respectively (Brill & McKeen 2024: 2–3). With regard to textual transmission, it is significant that women have been systematically excluded or marginalised from historical narratives about the development of Western philosophy in Greek and Roman antiquity; their contributions to this development have generally been over-looked.[16]

In attempting to factor in the impact of this marginalisation to our assessment of ancient women philosophers, some recent feminist scholarship is particularly useful. Miranda Fricker's work on epistemic injustice – specifically, hermeneutic and testimonial forms of injustice – raises the significant issue of the ways in which the social experiences of the oppressed and marginalised are not properly integrated into collective understandings of the world. She argues that ' ... any epistemic injustice wrongs someone in their capacity as a subject of knowledge ... the particular way in which testimonial injustice

---

[15] See McHardy & Marshall 2004: 2–3; McLaughlin 2004: 7–25.
[16] Brill & McKeen 2024: 6; O'Reilly & Pellò 2023: 2–3.

does this is that a hearer wrongs a speaker in his capacity as a giver of knowledge' (Fricker 2007: 5). This occurs when prejudice causes a hearer (or reader) to give a reduced level of credibility to a speaker's word (Fricker 2007: 1). With regard to epistemic injustice and the history of women in philosophy, this Element follows the approach of Sara Brill and Catherine MacKeen:

> ... the eclipsing and exclusion of women from scholarship in the history of philosophy is, among many other things, an ongoing instance of epistemic injustice. In investigating philosophy's past, then, we should be attentive to how epistemic privilege and epistemic disadvantage shaped contemporaneous collective understandings of Greek social-cultural worlds, and thus how these forces continue to limit our understanding of antiquity. We should test methods that have the potential to redress the long-standing epistemic injustices which have been inscribed into the history of philosophy. (Brill & McKeen 2024: 4)

Of course, the modern philosophical canon partially results from contingency since historical accidents have sometimes 'determined which texts survive and which do not' (Brill & McKeen 2024: 5). But the formation of the canon (as well as historical narratives about philosophy) is also, at least partially, the result of choice and selection. We have to recognise that the philosophical canon 'was formed in response to the concerns of specific times and places and was formulated in relation to local biases, prejudices and blind-spots'.[17] Thus, consideration of traditions of textual transmission is significant, especially when examining ancient women's philosophical writings and their lack of survival (see Section 4). Sara Brill and Catherine McKeen note that in applying these insights of feminist epistemology to the history of ancient philosophy, it is crucial to 'think from the margins', that is, 'to take as central the experiences of those who occupy less privileged and powerful social positions' (Brill & McKeen 2024: 5). Since women in antiquity were not a homogenous group, we must also consider the intersectional dimensions of citizen/immigrant and elite/non-elite (Brill & McKeen 2024: 5). Focusing on women's agency offers one of many possible correctives to the epistemic injustice that has marginalised the intellectual contributions and attainments of ancient women. As such, this study argues that the existing evidence allows us to glimpse a much wider pattern of female philosophical activity within the Platonic tradition than is usually recognised and that we should be careful not to underestimate or minimise the roles and philosophical activities of ancient women within the history of Platonism.

---

[17] Brill & McKeen 2024: 5. See Hutton 2015: 10.

Agency refers to the ability to act and to make independent choices. Accordingly, this Element aims to focus on women's attested intellectual activities and roles, specifically as philosophical teachers and students (Sections 2 and 3), writers of philosophical texts (Section 4), 'philosopher-priestesses' (Section 5) and, overall, as transmitters of philosophical knowledge and ritual expertise. It is also important to acknowledge and draw out more relational, collective and instrumental forms of agency, which focus on actions and interventions relating to means, instrumentality and mediation: these forms of agency pay attention to the individual's embeddedness within social, intellectual and cultural contexts and their capacity to act within these contexts.[18] To focus on instrumental and relational forms of agency allows the present work to explore women's roles (1) in catalysing or inspiring the production of male-authored philosophical works; (2) as empowered and empowering role models and (3) as catalytic forces for philosophical schools and communities. Focusing on women's agency in these senses (active, relational, collective and instrumental) may also reflect the qualities cultivated by Platonist philosophers themselves as central to philosophical practice: on the one hand, self-sufficiency and independence of mind and, on the other, the care for and connection with others considered vital for philosophical development and especially for the cultivation of the virtues.

Examining women's roles in the transmission of philosophical knowledge and expertise, and their broader roles and activities within Platonist philosophical schools and communities, is essential for recovering their agency. By transmission, I refer to:

(1) Inter-generational transmission from teacher (formal or informal) to student. In terms of gender, this type of transmission in the Platonic tradition is usually male to female or female to male (as well as male to male), but there are traces of female-to-female transmission evident which are explored here too;

(2) Longer-term transmission of exemplary role models. Turning the lens on the transmission of philosophical knowledge facilitates the consideration of

---

[18] For a critique of traditional formulations of agency in relation to ancient women and discussion of relational and collective notions of agency, see Frank *et al.* (2024): 1–8. On instrumental agency, see Keller 2002: 59–61, who criticises post-Enlightenment constructions of agency and the 'agent' which construe the latter as a wholly autonomous and independent subject. She uses instrumental agency to re-assess women's roles within a diverse range of religious contexts, stating that instrumentality refers to the power of receptivity, comparable metaphorically to a flute or other instrument that is played, while agency implies action and a place where exchanges occur. Applying instrumental agency to ancient female philosophers draws on Keller's conception but relates this notion to women's social and intellectual roles and actions embedded within philosophical communities.

philosophical women as active agents and as part of a much wider picture of female involvement in ancient Platonist philosophical practice.

Focusing on these modes of transmission, Sections 2 and 3 explore women's roles in the world of Plato and later Platonism chronologically, while Sections 4 and 5 are thematic, focusing on women's involvement in textual production and their roles as philosopher-priestesses respectively.

2 Women in the World of Plato

While Plato's dialogues are dominated by male characters, several women feature indirectly in his works, with their speeches reported in flashback by Socrates. Women are also reported to have been female students in the Academy, where they studied under Plato and his successor, Speusippus. Plato's approach towards women is complex and ambiguous, compounded by the difficulty in ascertaining his views from his works, given the absence of authorial voice and use of the dialogue form. In the *Republic*, Plato's Socrates argues that natural talents are distributed among both genders; consequently, the ideal state should select women, as well as men, to act as Guardians and thus as 'philosopher queens'; women should be educated, trained and employed in the same areas as men, including in gymnastics, music and war, as well as philosophy (*Resp.* V, 451 c-466 c).[19] This was a radical stance for his time, even though this account contains many qualifications and pejorative remarks about women (for example, *Resp* V, 452b, 455d3-5). In other works, a less positive view of women is evident, such as in the *Timaeus*, where although the proposals regarding the equality of men and women are mentioned (*Ti.* 18 c), women are said to be reincarnations of men who were wicked or cowardly in their previous life (*Ti.* 90e-91a).[20] Cyril of Alexandria claims that Plato tried to win Dionysius' wife over to philosophy when he was staying at the latter's court in Sicily, though the equality of women in the *Republic* may have inspired this anecdote.[21]

In terms of social conditions and education, women in classical Athens could not vote or participate in politics, and were often associated with private rather than public life. However, gendered social protocols varied depending on age, class and status: for instance, some women, especially those from a non-elite background, were employed and left their homes for work (Blok 2001: 111).

---

[19] See Annas 1976; Garside Allen 1975: 131–138; Okin 1977: 345–369; O'Meara 2003: 83–86; Addey 2017: 412.
[20] See Blair 2012: 1–9, for discussion of the extensive scholarship on Plato's approach towards women.
[21] Cyril, *Adv. Iul.* 6.36,4. See Plato, *Epistle* 8.361a; Riginos 1976: 84.

Some women were doctors as well as midwives and participated in philosophical tradition in this capacity (Connell 2023: 57–76). In terms of education, girls and women were not educated publicly in classical Athens. Nonetheless, many Athenian vases (from the fifth century BCE onwards) show young girls learning how to read and citizen women studying book scrolls – almost as often as men and boys are depicted with book scrolls. This suggests that some girls from a wealthy background were educated, probably within their home or in small groups, under the direction of literate women (Dillon 2013: 396–408). Furthermore, caution is needed in determining if the educational and social patterns visible in classical Athens were identical or similar elsewhere in the Greek world. For example, in Sparta, the laws introduced by Lycurgus prescribed a public education for girls. Sparta is often seen as exceptional in this regard. However, it is possible that women from other regions of the Greek world may have received a more formal education: it is noticeable that the women who feature in Plato's dialogues or studied in his Academy, who were almost certainly literate and educated, come from regions of Greece outside of Athens and from Asia Minor.[22] It is likely that most regions lay somewhere between the extremes of Athens and Sparta with regard to education for women and social conditions. Certainly after the classical period, education for women expanded; several terracotta figurines (from the turn of the fourth century BCE) depict girls reading, writing and carrying writing tablets (Dillon 2013: 408).

2.1 Women in Plato's Works

In several works, Plato's Socrates presents didactic speeches delivered to him by women: Diotima and Aspasia, who feature in Plato's *Symposium* and *Menexenus* respectively. Since many scholars agree that Socrates is presented by Plato as the philosopher par excellence, it seems significant that Plato's Socrates claims that these women were his teachers and treats their teaching with great respect, even if Plato's depiction of Aspasia is contested. Plato also portrays Socrates listening to the prophetic message of the woman who appears in his dream (*Cri.* 44a5-b2) and framing the direction of his life, impetus to elenchus, and philosophical path as catalysed by the oracle delivered by the Pythia (*Ap.* 22a4, 23b4-c1, 33c5-9). Socrates alludes to the female lyric poet Sappho with admiration, describing her as 'wise' and 'lovely' (*Phaedr.* 235b6, c2-4).

---

[22] See D'Angour 2019: 193, on Aspasia's educational attainments and possible education in Miletus.

2.1.1 Diotima of Mantinea

Plato places one of his most important speeches in the mouth of Diotima, whose teaching Socrates reports in flashback during a symposium when it is his turn to give a speech on *erōs*, a term usually translated as 'love' but perhaps better translated as 'passionate attraction' or 'longing' (*Symp.* 201d-212a). Socrates claims that Diotima was his teacher and that he learned from her on several occasions, although the setting is not specified.[23] Socrates' contribution – consisting of his report of Diotima's teaching – is almost as long as all the other speeches in the work combined, and defines and gives new meaning to the roles of the 'philosopher' and 'philosophy' (Hadot 2002: 39–40).

In terms of the setting, the symposium was, in classical Athens, a male-dominated, homosocial environment attended by aristocratic men; usually the only women allowed to attend were female courtesans and entertainers who provided entertainment for the male guests. In Plato's *Symposium*, this male-dominated atmosphere is intensified, as the male characters discourse on the male vision of love and the homosexual relations between some of the male guests are presented openly.[24] The characters decide to send away the flute-girl – the only woman physically present at the dinner-party – so they can make speeches in praise of *erōs*.[25] Eryximachus suggests that she can play to the women in the women's quarters, raising the intriguing possibility that there is a female social gathering taking place simultaneously in another part of Agathon's household.[26] As such, a strict separation – along gender binary lines – of women and men in the physical setting of the dialogue is enacted.[27] Socrates' report of Diotima's discourse is radical in re-introducing a female voice and presence into the dinner-party and, even more significantly, into the intellectual discourse about *erōs* and, in a wider sense, into philosophical discourse. After Socrates reports Diotima's teaching, there is a knock on the door and the sounds of revellers and music (212c8-10): a drunken Alcibiades turns up and is 'brought into the company by the flute-girl' (212d7-8). Figuratively, Diotima's indirect presence (via Socrates' speech) seems to allow women – and the female – into the symposium and draws women into philosophy, implicitly challenging the exclusion and separation of women enacted earlier in the dialogue.

---

[23] *Symp.* 206b4-5, 207a6-7; Levin 1975: 229.   [24] Saxonhouse, 1984: 11; Halperin 1990: 257.
[25] *Symp.* 176e; Saxonhouse 1984: 11–12.
[26] Gilhuly 2008: 62–64. I thank Dawn LaValle Norman for discussion of this issue (personal correspondence, 22 April 2023).
[27] *Contra* Gilhuly 2008: 64, who argues that the flute-girl is present at the symposium to allow for the articulation of the separation of the feminine and philosophical discourse. This is certainly the case in Erixymachus' comment but Socrates' evocation of Diotima and her words challenges and dissolves this separation.

Plato's Socrates presents Diotima as a philosopher, priestess, seer and mystagogue from Mantinea. Her theophoric name means 'honouring Zeus' or 'honoured by Zeus'; Socrates introduces her by discussing her ritual service, reporting that she attained a delay to the onset of the plague by advising the Athenians to offer expiatory sacrifices (201d6-8). This ritual service marks Diotima as a seer. Her teaching is imbued with religious terminology and concepts; overall, she is presented as a paradigmatic philosopher-priestess, a theme examined in Section 5.

Some have argued that Diotima is not presented as a philosopher but as a sophist, partially because Socrates calls her 'wise' several times (201d3, 208b8) and on one occasion compares her to a sophist (208c1), but primarily due to the methods she uses in her discourse, making several long didactic speeches (203b1-204a7, 208c1-212a7) and sometimes answering her own questions rather than waiting for Socrates to answer.[28] In relation to this, Diotima's teaching uses a range of methods, including elenctic questioning, as well as didactic speeches and myth (which closely parallel Plato's wide range of methods and styles evident elsewhere in his dialogues), and Plato's Socrates himself makes two lengthy speeches in the *Phaedrus*. Moreover, Socrates' introductory description of Diotima as a 'wise woman' (σοφή) who is skilled concerning Eros and 'many other matters' (ἄλλα πολλά) (201d2-3) recalls his claim in Plato's *Meno* that he learnt many things from priests and priestesses (*Meno* 81a10-b1) whom he specifically designates 'wise men and women' (81a5-6: ἀνδρῶν τε καὶ γυναικῶν σοφῶν) who discuss 'divine matters' (θεῖα πράγματα). Rather than establishing her as a sophist, Diotima's longer speeches seemingly mark a change of register to a kind of oracular or initiatory mode of discourse (see Section 5.1).

Using elenctic questioning, Diotima refutes the younger Socrates' idea that Eros is a god by showing him that *erōs* involves a desire for what one lacks, a desire for beautiful and good things, whereas the gods lack nothing and are happy and beautiful. Rather, she draws out from Socrates the recognition that *erōs* must be intermediate. Diotima teaches Socrates about the nature of Eros, presenting him as a *daimōn*, a semi-divine being who is 'in between' (μεταξύ) god and human, immortal and mortal, beauty and ugliness, and knowledge and ignorance (201e10-202e5). Diotima locates Eros within the realm of *daimones*, who act as intermediaries between gods and mortals, transporting human prayers and offerings to the gods and divinatory messages from the gods to humans (202e5-203a9). She relates the myth of Eros' birth from his father, Plenty, and mother, Poverty, claiming Eros has the characteristics of both

---

[28] See Nails 2015: 80–82; Keime 2016: 384–385.

parents (203b1-e7). After this, Diotima reverts to elenctic questioning and enquires about the love of good things, drawing out from Socrates that everyone longs for good things and, consequently, happiness; this section culminates in the definition of love as all desire for good things and happiness (204d1-205d3). Since Diotima somewhat abruptly switches from investigating beauty to goodness (204e1-2), a contested issue is whether she equates goodness with beauty in treating them synonymously; at a minimum, she implies that they are closely connected.

After defining *erōs*, Diotima alludes explicitly to Aristophanes' earlier speech (189 c-193d), which related a cosmogonic myth to explain that love is the longing for one's 'other half' and thus a desire for wholeness. Aristophanes reported an origin myth of the human race, where humans originally existed in a self-sufficient state: they were spherical, with two faces and sets of genitals, and four ears and limbs (189e5-190a4). There were three genders: male, female and androgynous, relating to the participation of each in the sun, earth or moon (189d6-e4,190a8-b3). These spherical humans hubristically conspired to fight against the gods and Zeus punishes them by breaking them in two, with Apollo sewing up the cut to heal them (190b5-191a5). After this, each human was incomplete and there were two genders (male and female) rather than three. They longed for their 'other half' and ran to their matches, refusing to leave them, leading to inertia and starvation. The gods moved their genitals to the front, making the union of male and female generate offspring and making sexual union potentially generate satisfaction in a way that entailed lovers could separate temporarily to carry out other tasks (191a5-d3). Aristophanes comments that the original humans were dispersed by the god, just as the Arcadians had been dispersed by the Lacedaemonians (193a2-3), which may be an anachronistic allusion to Sparta's dispersal of Mantinea in 385 BCE (Corrigan & Glazov Corrigan 2004: 79).

Diotima's teaching encompasses the idea which first emerges in Aristophanes' speech that love or *erōs* is a longing or lack, an incompleteness, yet she reconfigures the goal and orientation of this longing. While Aristophanes' speech presented humans – and even the gods – as ultimately self-seeking, Diotima parodies and 'corrects' Aristophanes' idea that love is a longing for one's other half.[29] She argues that love is not a longing for another half or wholeness, but a desire for what is good. To do so, she uses the imagery of amputation drawn from Aristophanes' speech by giving the example of the willingness of humans to have their limbs amputated if these are considered

---

[29] See Corrigan & Glazov-Corrigan 2004: 70–80, on Aristophanes' portrayal of gods and humans as self-seeking.

harmful to their overall health (205d11-e7). She concludes the allusion with her argument that humans love the good (206a1). Later, Diotima's picture of the ascent to Beauty itself – the so-called 'ladder of love' – will present beauty and goodness as simultaneously transcendent and immanent, drawing humans to a greater reality which involves recognising the beauty and goodness of other beings and includes care and concern for others (208c1-212a7).[30] Diotima, as a Mantinean and Arcadian, has been symbolically 'dispersed' by Aristophanes' comparison, like his spherical humans in the myth (and like Dionysos), but she figuratively does the 'reconciliatory' and healing work of Apollo in reconfiguring the goal and direction of *erōs*: her account incorporates the idea of *erōs* as longing and lack but re-orients the direction of this longing towards the good, rather than wholeness.

Diotima's speech is especially important for – and even constitutive of – Plato's definition of the 'philosopher' and for his conception of philosophy; this definition of the 'philosopher' would become central in the subsequent history of philosophy (Hadot 2002: 39–40). The philosopher, or 'the follower of wisdom', is presented as intermediate between the wise and the ignorant, just as Eros is (203e6-204b5).[31] Crucially, Eros' intermediate nature in this respect comes from his parentage, with Poverty or lack being as crucial to the attainment of wisdom as Plenty is. Indeed, Diotima's mythical description applies equally to Eros, Socrates (as Plato's ideal philosopher) and the philosopher in broader terms (Hadot 2002: 43). In Plato's conception of philosophy, it is precisely our awareness of our *lack* of wisdom – and our longing (*erōs*) for it – that motivates our search for wisdom (204a2-b9). Thus, *erōs* is crucial for the philosopher, always questioning and searching for wisdom, and their philosophical path.

It is significant that both the content and the framing of Diotima's speech are infused with matters relating to gender. Through using elenchus, Diotima describes how love is love of good things and the method to attain what is genuinely good is 'the begetting on a beautiful thing by means of both body and soul' (206b9-10). Diotima argues that all humans who feel *erōs* desire to possess the beloved forever and thus aim for immortality through generation and procreation; her account here is remarkably inclusive, noting that even animals feel *erōs* for their beloved and children (204e1-209a1). Diotima

---

[30] See Sheffield 2006: 154–182, for examination of Diotima's teaching as necessarily involving care for others, because 'the mediatory nature of *erōs* suggests engagement with others in the role of guide. Contemplation of the form may not require another person, but our natures may require us to keep realizing that activity in our lives and to communicate back from the divine form to the realm of human concerns' (182).

[31] For an extended discussion, see Hadot 2002: 29, 39–51.

maintains that humans can become pregnant in soul as well as body, using pregnancy as an image for giving birth to the beautiful (209a1-e5). Then, Diotima traces an ascending path from loving a beautiful body to appreciating the beauty in all bodies, to loving the beauty of souls, to loving and appreciating the beauty of laws and institutions, through to loving all branches of knowledge, to contemplating the 'Beautiful' itself (i.e. the Form of Beauty) (209e6-212a10). Diotima presents this philosophical ascent in relational terms, catalysed by *erōs* and connecting the philosopher (in a cumulative sense) to beautiful people, phenomena, types of knowledge and, ultimately, to Beauty itself. Her discourse raises many questions about the nature of immortality. Some have argued that she excludes Plato's theory of the immortality of the soul by focusing on mortality and procreation as the means to a kind of immortality.[32] However, Diotima consistently speaks of 'mortal nature' (207d1-2: ἡ θνητὴ φύσις, which may refer specifically to the *mortal* elements of the human being) and maintains that 'a mortal thing participates in immortality' (208b2: θνητὸν ἀθανασίας μετέχει).[33] As such, her philosophy is deeply relational, encompassing every aspect of embodied life, including all that is mortal, as an intimation or echo of immortality because everything 'participates' in some way in the intelligible world of the Forms. Diotima's speech utilises the terminology of pregnancy, giving birth and (pro-)creation. This terminology is echoed in several of Plato's works, suggesting its importance for his philosophical project. In the *Phaedrus*, Socrates speaks of 'impregnating minds' and of 'sowing discourses which themselves contain a seed from which, in other natures, will grow other discourses capable ... of leading us to the highest degree of happiness possible for human beings' (*Phaedr.* 277a). In the *Theaetetus*, Socrates compares his philosophical practice, specifically his elenctic method of questioning and drawing out wisdom from others, to midwifery (*Tht.* 149a-151d). He begins this comparison by alluding to his mother, Phaenarete, and her role as a midwife, stating that he practises the same art (*Tht.* 149a1-4). Socrates connects this role with the roots of his philosophical mission at the behest of Apollo's oracle as described in the *Apology*: 'the god compels me to act as a midwife'.[34] Socrates' use of the midwifery image seems to suggest that his philosophical practice is concerned with 'a relational approach to ideas embedded in the care of other's souls; his

---

[32] See, for example, Nails 2015: 82–83.
[33] Dover (1965: 16–20) interprets θνητὸν ἀθανασίας μετέχει, καὶ σῶμα καὶ τἆλλα πάντα as 'both a mortal body and all else [that is mortal]' (17) and demonstrates convincingly that Diotima does not necessarily exclude the survival of the soul, even if her account does not focus on this idea.
[34] *Tht.* 150c7-8. See also 150d4-5, 150d8-e1, 151b4. On Apollo's oracle as the catalyst for Socrates' philosophical practice, see Section 1.1.2.

use of this image to describe his relations to others, emphasises a feminine quality to his philosophical approach' (McCoy 2024: 254).

As noted, David Halperin (1990: 257–299) argues that Plato uses Diotima to appropriate the feminine into his account of male *erōs* since the latter is presented as requiring reciprocal and (pro-)creative characteristics which, in classical Athens, were associated with women and the feminine. In his view, Diotima – as a woman – is used to facilitate Plato's account of *erōs* as a male, homosocial concern. Frisbee Sheffield (2023: 21–37) has effectively refuted Halperin's argument by demonstrating that Diotima's account of *erōs*, with its educational aspirations and focus, applies to *all* human beings (πάντες ἄνθρωποι, *Symp.* 206c1-2), who are, despite the homoerotic context of some sections of her speech, ' . . . pregnant in both body and soul and enabled by *erōs* in their creative endeavours as they strive to create a life worth living' (Sheffield 2023: 26). Furthermore, what Halperin had argued was 'gender-polarised' vocabulary in Diotima's speech is – in relation to Greek culture – predominantly gender-neutral. Terms relating to conception, pregnancy and childbirth in the speech can apply to both sexes: for example, the term *kueo* (209a1, a2, b1, b5, c3) can mean 'conceive' (in the sense that a woman conceives a child) but with a male subject, it means 'impregnate'. *Tikto,* to 'bring into the world' or 'engender', used of a female subject means 'bear' but of a male subject means 'beget' (Evans 2006: 14; Sheffield 2023: 29–30). As Frisbee Sheffield argues, 'the philosophical point . . . is that physical pregnancy is but one species of a much larger phenomenon, which covers human creativity of all kinds' (Sheffield 2023: 30, citing *Symp.* 205b7-c3). Moreover, the very first thing that Diotima teaches Socrates is the importance of moving beyond binary thinking: just as Eros lies 'in between' god and human, immortal and mortal, and wisdom and ignorance – and indeed, lies intermediate between all opposites – so the philosopher too has to move beyond binary oppositions and categorisations. As such, Plato's Diotima implicitly problematises and challenges the conceptualisation of gender as a binary opposition (Sheffield 2023: 22). In doing so, Diotima's discourse reverses or 'corrects' the direction of Aristophanes' speech, which had concluded with the dispersal of the androgynous and left humans gendered in a binary fashion (male and female).

Diotima's identity is contested, specifically whether she was a historical figure or a fictitious character invented by Plato, since she only features in Plato's *Symposium* (later sources which mention her derive from Plato's account) and we (currently) have no independent evidence attesting to her existence. It has become conventional to assume that Diotima is fictitious, even though the question of her identity is inconclusive based on current evidence.³⁵ Arguments supporting this apparent fictionality are rarely stated although Diotima's allusion to the content of Aristophanes' speech in the *Symposium* has been interpreted as supporting the idea that her speech could not have been composed long before the dinner-party, given the anachronism (Nehamas & Woodruff 1989: xii). However, Aristophanes' speech also seems to contain an anachronism about the Arcadians: the philosophical and dramatic effects of this possible use of anachronism in both speeches may be to draw attention to their interconnections in terms of the ideas about love expressed therein. Furthermore, there may be no anachronism in Diotima's teaching since the myth on which Aristophanes' speech is based on may derive from a lost play (Nails 2002: 138). This seems likely given that several of Aristophanes' extant plays focus on gender and sexuality, such as the *Lysistrata* and *Ecclesiazusiae*. It may be relevant that Aristophanes' *Birds* also contains a cosmogonic myth, told from the perspective of the birds tracing their genealogy from Eros (693-703). It seems significant that Aristophanes is introduced by Socrates as someone whose vital occupation concerns Dionysos and Aphrodite (*Symp.* 177d-e), with the latter suggestive of the idea that his plays often deal with issues relating to love, gender or sexuality (see Santoro 2016: 214). Alternatively, Aristophanes' speech may have a precedent in mythology unknown to us (Nails 2002: 138), possibly relating to popular Greek folklore (Dover 1966: 45). Aristophanes' speech contains allusions to the evolutionary theories of Empedocles and may represent a parody of Orphic myths and theogonies.³⁶

Overall, there are good reasons for holding that Diotima may well have been a historical figure.³⁷ Indeed, the vast majority of characters in Plato's dialogues are based on historical figures (Nails 2015: 74). Of the named characters, only three are unattested in historical sources of evidence from Plato's time or earlier: Timaeus of Locris, Callicles of Athens and Diotima (Levin 1975: 224). In the case of Diotima and Timaeus, whose provenance is non-Athenian, these figures would be less likely to show up in the extant historical record given that so much of our evidence for classical Greece comes from Athens (Levin 1975: 225). Some have argued that Diotima is modelled on or stands in for Aspasia of Miletus, primarily because they contend that Plato transforms Aeschines' focus on Socratic erotic discourse as set out in his dialogue *Aspasia* (Halperin 1990). Armand D'Angour has recently argued that Diotima is a code-name for Aspasia (D'Angour 2019: 38–44; 197–203). While it seems reductive to reduce the two women who feature in Plato's works to one historical figure, this argument is

---

[35] See Nails 2002: 137; Nye 2015: x–xii, 2–6.
[36] Corrigan & Glazov Corrigan 2004: 70; Santoro 2016: 218-225.
[37] Kranz 1926: 437; Nails 2015: 73.

more persuasive than the notion that Diotima was entirely fictitious, although it is still circumstantial and inconclusive.

Symbolically, Socrates' reporting of Diotima's speech seems to facilitate the presence of women into the conversation about *erōs,* and into philosophy itself, as well as the physical space of the symposium, reminding the guests – and the reader – that philosophy and culture are for everyone, regardless of gender. Diotima's speech itself challenges gender binaries and seems to present an inclusive view of philosophy as a *human,* rather than gendered, endeavour. Diotima's teaching is inclusive in a cosmic and metaphysical sense, encouraging the aspiring philosopher to move beyond all binary ways of thinking about reality, and including all living beings (non-human animals as well as humans) in the experience of *erōs* and (pro-)creation.

2.1.2 Aspasia of Miletus

Aspasia (born late 470s BCE) was important in the intellectual history of fifth-century Athens and in Greek philosophical dialogue.[38] She was one of the most controversial figures in classical Athens, largely because she was the long-term partner of Pericles, the leading statesman in Athens at the time, for about twenty years from sometime after 450 to 429 BCE (Nails 2002: 59). Aspasia came from an aristocratic background and was highly educated: she was associated with the Socratic circle, including Socrates himself, and had a reputation as a teacher and rhetorician.[39] Born in Miletus, Aspasia was the daughter of Axiochus of Miletus; she came to Athens with her sister and brother-in-law, Alcibiades II, in the 450s (Nails 2002: 59). The latter was the grandfather of the (in)famous Alcibiades and so Aspasia was a distant relative of the Alcibiades who features in Plato's *Symposium* (Henry 1995: 10–11). Although Aspasia can tentatively be identified as the relative of an Athenian aristocrat, she was also a resident alien – a metic – a status characterised by many liabilities (Henry 1995: 11–13). In particular, Aspasia arrived in Athens soon after the passing of the citizenship law of 451/450 BCE which restricted Athenian citizenship to persons with two Athenian parents and entailed that non-Athenian women, like Aspasia, could not enter fully valid Athenian marriages (Henry 1995: 12).

Aspasia's significance is evident in the many attacks on her by comic playwrights, who often mocked the leading figures in Athens. However, Aspasia was treated very differently from the leading men portrayed: comic

---

[38] On Aspasia, see especially Henry 1995; Nails 2002: 58–62. Aspasia's date of death is uncertain: Nails 2002: 58, places it before 401 BCE.

[39] For a collection of fragments of Socratic texts attesting Aspasia, see Boys-Stones & Rowe 2013: 233–252.

allusions to her attack her as a prostitute and procuress, and 'are invariably sexual, sexualized and sexualizing' (Henry 1995: 19).[40] It is often assumed that Aspasia was a courtesan (*hetaira*), since Plutarch describes her as such (*Pericles* 24.5-6), yet she is not described in this way by her contemporaries.[41] Since courtesans enjoyed more independence than most groups of women in classical Athens, and had a reputation for their intellectual and cultural conversation, this is possible, but it is difficult to ascertain if this reputation has any historical basis or rather reflects misogynistic abuse aimed at a woman who dared to mix freely with men in intellectual circles.

Aspasia's impact on the Socratic circle was considerable: she features in many of the dialogues authored by Socrates' companions in the fourth century BCE. Although she does not appear as a character in her own right, two of them bore her name – Aeschines and Antisthenes both write dialogues entitled *Aspasia*. Only a few fragments of Antisthenes' dialogue survive, all of which mention Aspasia's relationship with Pericles or attack Pericles' family (Boys-Stones & Rowe 2013: 240–241). The general consensus is that Antisthenes treats her unfavourably (Henry 1995: 30–32). The surviving fragments of Aeschines' work indicate a more positive portrayal: there is a focus on Aspasia's wisdom, political expertise and sharp wit (Aeschines fr. 60). Socrates recommends Aspasia as a teacher for Callias' son, when asked for a recommendation. When Callias balks at the idea of a female teacher, Socrates recounts tales of famous women from the past, such as the Persian queen Rhodogyne and Thargelia, an Ionian woman associated with powerful men. Aeschines presents Aspasia as 'philosophizing with Socrates' and was the first ancient writer to show Aspasia in a manner which suggests that *erōs* and the search for *arete* (virtue) are intertwined, in a scene where she questions and advises Xenophon and his wife on marriage.[42] In Xenophon's works, Aspasia is depicted as an expert in matchmaking and relationships (*Mem.* 2.6.36; *Oec.*3.14).

Most significantly for our purposes, Aspasia features indirectly in Plato's *Menexenus* when Socrates reports a speech composed by her, showing that Plato's use of Aspasia was an important exception to her limited role in earlier Socratic dialogues. The work consists of opening and closing dialogues between Socrates and Menexenus (*Menex.* 234a-236d, 249d-e), with a funeral speech attributed to Aspasia (236d-249 c) placed between these frames. The

---

[40] On the depiction of Aspasia in Old Comedy, see Henry 1995: 19–28.
[41] In Old Comedy, Aspasia was called a 'concubine' (*pallakē*) (which Henry 1995: 21 argues reflects the nature of her relationship with Pericles) and a 'prostitute' (*pornē*); both terms have different connotations from *hetaira*.
[42] Aeschines fr. 60, 66, 70, in Boys-Stones & Rowe 2013: 234–237; Henry 1995: 40–41.

dialogue begins with Socrates talking to a young man, Menexenus, who has come from the Council Chamber where the Athenians are selecting a speaker to praise the war dead.[43] The short sections of dialogue between them at the beginning and end of the work highlight gender issues, as well as offering reflections on the art of oratory. Socrates introduces Aspasia as his, and Pericles I's, teacher (διδάσκαλος) in oratory, and praises her compositions.[44] Socrates presents Aspasia as one of his main teachers, alongside Connus who had instructed him in the arts (235e9-236a1), and says that he heard her composing a speech in praise of the war dead yesterday, creating it from a patchwork of improvised sections and parts from the speech that she had prepared when composing the funeral oration which Pericles delivered (236b6-7). Thus, Socrates attributes the composition of Pericles' famous funeral oration to her. After Socrates reports Aspasia's speech, Menexenus expresses doubt twice about Aspasia's intellectual abilities, her oratorical skills and her composition, because she is a woman (249d3-4, 249d11-e2).

The *Menexenus* is one of Plato's strangest dialogues; interpretations of the work are diverse, including reading it as a mocking parody, a ghost story, or as a philosophically improved version of a funeral speech. Because the funeral speech narrates Athenian events down to 386 BCE, there is an anachronism because Socrates – and presumably Aspasia – had been dead for more than a decade by this time. Bruce Rosenstock argues that this makes the work a dialogue between ghosts, with Socrates and Aspasia appearing as shades, a reading which resonates with a recurring theme of the work: souls crossing the border between life and death (Rosenstock 1994: 288–300). This reading also considers Menexenus (usually assumed to be Socrates' friend who appears in the *Lysis*) to be Socrates' son – who would have been a young man in 386, but would have been too young to be taught by Socrates during the latter's lifetime – whom the shade of Socrates advises as he comes of age.[45] Danielle Layne reads the dialogue as depicting ancestral wisdom transmitted though father and mother, with the latter embodied by Aspasia, in a kind of daimonic remembrance on the part of Menexenus as he invokes the daimonic advice of his long-passed father, and is exhorted 'by a thoughtful mother to remember and hold dear his ancestors, all those who bequeathed to him a virtuous life more valuable than any reputation. This is the life which always remembers that the goddess safeguards the voices and wisdom of those who most justly adorn her, as they need not lament the loss of either father or mother. Due to their philosophical

---

[43] On the *epitaphios*, the funeral oration over the war dead peculiar to Athens, see Thomas 1989: 196–237.
[44] *Menex.* 235e6, 236a1. See Nails 2002: 60.
[45] Rosenstock 1994: 339; Dean-Jones 1995: 51–57.

"education" and corresponding care or "nurture" they remain very much alive' (Layne 2026: 21–22).

Ancient tradition focused on the content of the funeral speech in this work, regarded as the *epitaphos* par excellence: Cicero reports it was so popular that it was recited annually in Athens during the Hellenistic and Roman periods (*Orat.* 151). Despite this, the orthodox interpretation of the speech is that it is a satirical parody of the genre of the funeral oration which Plato uses to criticise rhetoric.[46] Drawing on the introductory conversation, many scholars have interpreted the speech as a mocking parody, because Socrates seems to disparage oratory, alerting the reader to the possibility of irony and satire.[47] Nicole Loraux argues that the attribution of the speech to Aspasia – a woman and foreigner – indicates that it is a parody, since silence was expected of women in classical Athens and the introduction of a feminine element into an overwhelmingly male procedure effectively discredits the oration (Loraux 1986: 323). Yet there are surviving examples of Athenian funeral orations (sample speeches written before Plato's *Menexenus*) composed by Gorgias and Lysias, neither of whom was an Athenian citizen; indeed, Lysias was a metic in Athens like Aspasia (Pappas & Zelcer 2015: 61–63). Although the prologue of the work has a playful tone, it is far from clear that such playfulness signifies irony or mockery, given that Plato suggests elsewhere that playfulness is the opposite of solemnity rather than seriousness (*Resp.* 536e, 424d). The depiction of Aspasia within this work is, in many ways, playful and ambivalent (Robitzsch 2017).

Nickolas Pappas and Mark Zelcer have argued convincingly that the *Menexenus* sets out an improved version of a funeral oration, the kind of speech a philosopher would give to educate citizens in developing virtue, given the emphasis on education within the speech and framing sections (Pappas & Zelcer 2015). They note that 'the ends and means of education as presented in the *Menexenus* overlap with the ends and means of education as the *Republic* conceives that process', including tutelage in political leadership, military training, learning from beneficent deities and the imitation (*mimesis*) of good models in order to develop virtue (Pappas & Zelcer 2015: 97–99). On this basis, they argue that the speech in the *Menexenus* depicts philosophy bringing a pedagogical impulse to funeral rhetoric that the *Republic* says philosophical rulers would bring to all aspects of governing a city (Pappas & Zelcer 2015: 99). Since women are explicitly included in education, philosophy and politics in the *Republic*, Plato's attribution of the speech to Aspasia may evoke (in practical, concrete terms) the capacities of women with regard to philosophy and political

---

[46] See Henry 1995; Thomas 1989: 196–237; Loraux 1986: 8–9, 265–270.
[47] See Thomas 1989: 210–211, citing *Menex.* 234c, 235a, 235d, 236a.

leadership – thus, Aspasia may be presented as a kind of 'prototype' philosopher-queen in the *Menexenus*. Aspasia's mastery of traditionally 'male' spheres of activity (rhetoric, political debate) may reflect the qualities Plato envisages in female Guardians. Plato certainly challenges Socratic depictions of Aspasia by taking her out of the domestic realm with its emphasis on marriage (areas traditionally associated with women in classical Greece) and placing her within what was considered a male sphere – that of politics and rhetoric (Pappas & Zelcer 2015: 36). Within the opening and closing frames, Plato explicitly raises gender issues which correspond closely to what we would now call 'epistemic injustice': he characterises Menexenus as an ambitious young man concerned with civic and business affairs, who takes the speech to be a parody (235c6) and repeatedly doubts Aspasia's intellectual and oratorical abilities because she is a woman (249d3-4, d11-e2). However, Socrates calls Menexenus incompletely educated and casts doubt on his grasp of philosophy.[48] In the concluding section, Socrates challenges Menexenus' treatment of Aspasia, inviting him to visit her and see her talents for himself (249d6-7). Furthermore, Socrates treats Aspasia with great respect in the dialogue. If we take Socrates as representative of the philosopher par excellence for Plato and pay attention to characterisation within the work, then Plato may be depicting Aspasia as the embodiment – or at least a concrete example – of the capacities of women to engage in philosophy, political leadership and rhetoric, a kind of female Guardian in action.

Overall, Aspasia had a considerable impact on the Socratic circle and is fairly consistently presented by Plato and the Socratics as a teacher and rhetorician. Aspasia features in many sources but her presentation is constantly refracted through the male gaze: we hear more about her sexual status and controversial relationship with Pericles than about her intellectual activities. Consequently, it is difficult to say anything definitive about her intellectual attainments. However, the overall impression from the sources is that Aspasia was a woman who refused to observe the gendered protocols of classical Athens and thus chose to subvert the patriarchal restrictions placed upon women to a large extent. She conversed with and may have taught Socrates and others linked with the Socratics on her own terms. Although we do not know how the misogynistic abuse she received affected her personally, Aspasia seems to have refused to let it obstruct her intellectual activities.

---

[48] *Menex.* 234a4-6. See Pappas & Zelcer 2015: 91, who note this is the only appearance of the term *philosophia* in the dialogue.

2.2 Female Students in Plato's Academy

We have evidence that women were students in Plato's Academy. Diogenes Laertius (3.46) mentions them when listing Plato's most famous students, including Xenocrates, Aristotle and Philip of Opus: '... among them were two women, Lastheneia of Mantinea and Axiothea of Phlius, the latter of whom wore men's clothes, as Dicaerchus reports'. Although Diogenes' work is late (third century CE), he explicitly cites Dicearchus as his source, which strengthens the historical reliability of this evidence given that the latter was a pupil of Aristotle who lived and worked during the late fourth century BCE.[49] Diogenes reports that Axiothea and Lastheneia also studied under Speusippus, Plato's successor as Head of the Academy after the latter's death in 347 BCE (D.L. 4.2). Plato's women students were the focus of intense interest in antiquity and are mentioned in a wide range of sources; one of them (whose name is missing due to a lacuna in the text) was even mentioned in a papyrus from Oxyrynchus in Egypt, which reports that she studied philosophy with Plato and, after the latter's death, with Speusippus and then Menedemus of Eretria.[50]

Dicearchus (and Diogenes) reports that Axiothea dressed in men's clothes, a detail also mentioned in several later sources, some of which attribute this mode of dress to Lastheneia as well.[51] Whether this involved fully dressing in male clothing is uncertain: Philodemus indicates that it may have simply involved wearing a philosopher's cloak (τρίβων), a garment associated with Socrates, although the text is corrupt and uncertain.[52] If this text is historically accurate, Axiothea may have simply wanted to dress as a *philosopher* rather than as a man. This would make sense since the *tribon* was originally Spartan dress (Pappas & Zelcer 2015: 24) and Phlius, Axiothea's home-town, was under Spartan control. However, the philosopher's cloak was probably considered 'male clothing' in Athens at the time since male philosophers predominantly wore this garment and philosophy itself was often coded as a masculine activity in classical Athens. Interestingly, the same text mentions Axiothea's wisdom and skill in speculation as equal to that of a man.

If Axiothea dressed fully in male clothing, it is unclear whether she (and possibly Lastheneia) did so in order to fit into the public, homosocial and

---

[49] Dicaearchus, fr. 44 (Wehrli) (fl. 320–300 BCE).

[50] *P. Oxy* 3656, Col. 2, 1-19 in Dorandi 1989: 53, 63 (T8). For a collection of sources relating to Axiothea and Lastheneia, see Dorandi 1989. On Diogenes' female patron, see Section 3.

[51] Themistius, *Or.* 23.295c in Dorandi 1989. Sources which report both 'women' (γυναῖκες) dressing in men's clothes to study with Plato: Philodemus, *Academica* VI.26-2 in Kalligas et al. 2020; Olympiodorus, *In Platonis Alcibiadem commentaria* 2.147-50 in Dorandi 1989.

[52] Philodemus, *Academica, P Herc.* 1021 Y37-2,1. The reconstruction of the text is that of Gaiser 1988: 154–157, who argued that the passage is derived from Dicearchus. On Socrates' *tribon*, see Plato, *Symp.* 219b.

male-dominated environment of Plato's Academy, or, in a broader sense, to adhere to the tightly controlled gendered social restrictions of classical Athens, or possibly as a way of expressing a non-binary identity. However, it is likely that she did so in order to study safely and avoid unwanted male attention (including sexual advances and misogynistic abuse) in the male-dominated environment of the Academy and, in a broader sense, in classical Athens (Baltes 1993: 110). After all, many Athenians of the time, possibly including some of Plato's male students, considered women inferior to men and dismissed their capacity for intellectual work. It is probable that Axiothea and Lastheneia were aware, at least to some degree, of the treatment of Aspasia, a non-Athenian woman like themselves, who had faced considerable misogynistic abuse and hostility in Athens. As discussed previously, Aspasia had been endlessly mocked by Athenian comic playwrights (Henry 1995: 19–28). While these misogynistic attacks related largely to suspicion over her relationship with – and influence on – Pericles, Aspasia's public teaching and association with male Socratics probably contributed to this hostility. Within a wider context, it has been noted that female philosophers and intellectuals were often treated with suspicion for the very fact of mixing with male philosophers whom they were not necessarily related to and that the focus on their sexuality and sexual behaviour – including allegations that they were 'courtesans' – may well have stemmed from this misogynistic suspicion. Diogenes Laertius discusses a letter which Dionysius II of Syracuse had sent to Speusippus criticising the philosopher for charging fees for teaching which states, 'From the Arcadian woman who is your student one can grasp your wisdom' (D.L. 4.2), which refers to Lastheneia and either implies that Speusippus had an affair with her or, more generally, may be a misogynistic comment about teaching women. Athenaeus later cites this letter, claiming that Dionysius criticises Speusippus for his proneness to pleasure and love for Lastheneia, whom Athenaeus calls an 'Arcadian courtesan'. There is a parallel with Epicurean women philosophers who were often labelled 'courtesans' by critics intending to undermine the focus on pleasure within Epicurean ethics (Arenson 2023: 77–95). This tradition shows the constant suspicion, hostility and misogynistic abuse that women in classical Athens faced when studying philosophy alongside male students.[53]

As well as reporting that Axiothea disguised her sex, Themistius (*Or.* 23.295 c) adds that she was inspired to join Plato's school by reading his writings on the state, referring to the *Republic*. In the same passage, he mentions the protreptic effect of Plato's *Gorgias* on a Corinthian farmer who was inspired

---

[53] On Speusippus' affair with Lastheneia as part of a hostile tradition, see Baltes 1993: 12; Nails 2002: 2271; Dillon 2003: 32.

by this work to study with Plato, an anecdote also discussed by Aristotle in his Corinthian dialogue (Dorandi 1989: 56). This suggests that the account of the protreptic effect of the *Republic* on Axiothea derives from a much earlier source, thus strengthening its possible historical reliability. Scholars have contested whether Plato is committed to the equality of women in the *Republic* and whether he can be considered a 'proto-feminist', especially since he does not seem to seek to empower women for their own sake but to utilise their talents for the state.[54] However, the protreptic effect of the *Republic* in inspiring Axiothea to study with Plato is remarkable and suggests the influence of this work on Plato's female contemporaries in encouraging their involvement in philosophy.[55] Indeed, this anecdote may relate to the broader reasons for women's engagement with Plato's philosophy specifically, rather than with alternative philosophical movements. In the *Republic*, Plato's Socrates argues that women should be educated and trained in the same areas as men, including in music, gymnastics and warfare, as well as philosophy, so that they too can specialise in the type of work for which they are best suited (*Resp.* V, 451e-452a6, 453a1-b5). Therefore, the ideal state should select women, as well as men, to act as Guardians (V, 451c4-d11, 456a10-457c2). Consequently, Plato's Socrates advocates for the important role of 'philosopher queens' as well as philosopher-kings in the ideal state on the basis that the only differences between women and men are reproductive, which are not relevant to the tasks of Guardianship; rather, capacities and talents are distributed among *both* women and men (V, 451c4-11, 454c6-455e1). While many remarks in the *Republic* and *Timaeus* are more pejorative and cast doubt on the equal status of women, Plato's inclusion of women in philosophy and within the public sphere was radical for his time and likely resonated with women who were his contemporaries and those in subsequent periods who engaged with his philosophy. Indeed, Plato's *Republic*, including its defence of philosophical training for women, has been particularly influential and was read widely in late antiquity, the medieval period, the Renaissance and the early modern period.[56] Moreover, since Plato's women students were the focus of intense interest in antiquity, they almost certainly acted as philosophical role models for future generations of women who were involved in the Platonic tradition.

---

[54] See, for example, Pomeroy 1974; Annas 1976.
[55] For different interpretations of this anecdote, see Riginos 1976: 184 (no. 134); Wehrli 1967: 55.
[56] See Adamson 2023: 228–246, who examines the reception of Plato's account of women in the *Republic* in late antique Athens (Proclus), medieval Islamic Spain (Ibn Rushd) and the Italian Renaissance (Lucrezia Marinella). Plato's *Republic* remains well-known in contemporary times; it is often taught as a core text in universities to undergraduates in classics, philosophy, literature and politics.

The precise arrangements for and dynamics of Plato's teaching within the Academy are somewhat uncertain. He lived and taught in a private house in the Academy grounds, but also taught publicly in the park/gymnasia (D.L. 3.5). There seem to have been two gradations of students: an 'outer' circle of casual students who sought to understand the basics of philosophy, and an inner group of core students devoted to pursuing philosophy who were often researchers and teachers (Baltes 1993: 11). There is some evidence that Plato occasionally gave lectures to the public. It seems that Plato taught the inner group of students in the garden of his private house, while teaching the outer circle of hearers in the public spaces of the Academy.[57] We do not know which group of students Axiothea and Lastheneia belonged to, but the anecdote(s) about Axiothea – and Lastheneia – wearing male clothing implies that they started out as part of the outer group who studied in the Academy's public areas. The duration and longevity of their studies under both Plato and Speusippus suggests that both women became part of the inner group devoted to philosophy.

The geographical origins of Plato's female students are also potentially significant: Phlius and Mantinea are in the Peloponnese, so Axiothea and Lastheneia travelled a considerable distance to study with Plato. Indeed, many of Plato's students came from other regions of the eastern Mediterranean and were attracted by his reputation to travel to Athens to study with him.[58] Lastheneia is said to be from Mantinea, in Arcadia, and it is especially interesting that Iamblichus (*VP* 267) mentions 'Lastheneia from Arcadia' in his *Catalogue* of Pythagoreans which includes seventeen of the 'most famous' Pythagorean women.[59] There is consensus that Iamblichus' *Catalogue* originated in the fourth century BCE and is probably derived from Aristoxenus.[60] Some have argued that there is confusion between the Pythagorean and Platonic traditions within the biographical tradition: Fritz Wehrli (1967: 55) argues that the two women pupils are taken from the Pythagorean tradition and adopted by the Platonic, while Riginos (1976: 184, n.14) argues that the Pythagorean Lastheneia is more likely to be taken from the Platonic tradition, given that she is mentioned as early as Dicaearchus; if there is such confusion, the latter explanation is more probable.

However, the duplication of Lastheneia's name in the Pythagorean *Catalogue*, taken together with the geographical provenance of both women, may indicate Axiothea's and Lastheneia's involvement with local Pythagorean groups in their home-towns prior to studying with Plato and may suggest that

---

[57] Baltes 1993: 7; Watts 2007: 108.   [58] Baltes 1993: 11; Watts 2007: 110.
[59] For detailed examination of the *Catalogue* see Caterina Pellò's Element in this series (2022: 16 with n.44); Zhmud 2012: 111–119.
[60] Zhmud 2012: 111–119; Pellò 2022: 17–20.

those associated with the Pythagoreans (after Pythagoras' death and during Plato's lifetime) also in some cases studied with Plato, illustrating the close interconnections and shared philosophical commitments of Plato's circle and the Pythagoreans (Addey 2017: 418).[61] After all, Axiothea's home town, Phlius, marks the outer setting and framework of Plato's *Phaedo* – the fictitious venue of the dialogue is likely the gathering-place of the Pythagoreans in Phlius and the Pythagorean Echecrates asks Phaedo to tell them about Socrates' death.[62] Within this work and in Aristoxenus' list, Phlius is said to be home to a group of Pythagoreans (*Phd.* 57a7-8; Aristoxenus, fr. 11 in D.L. 8.46).[63] Phlius was a centre of Pythagoreanism on the Greek mainland from at least the late fifth or early fourth century BCE onwards, following the geographical dispersion of Pythagoreans after the anti-Pythagorean rebellions in Southern Italy.[64] The chronology would fit given that Aristoxenus (born ca. 370) was acquainted with pupils of Philolaus and Eurytus, counting them among the last Pythagoreans: these included Echecrates, Phanton, Diocles and Polymnastus who were in Phlius by the first half of the fourth century BCE (Riedwig 2002: 105), as well as Xenophilus, from which it follows that some Pythagoreans were still around on the Greek mainland in 350 BCE (Zhmud 2012: 63, 108). We do not know when Axiothea and Lasthenaia travelled to Athens and joined the Academy, but since they studied under both Plato and Speusippus, they were in Athens at some stage before 347 BCE and may well have been members of Pythagorean circles in the decades prior to this.[65]

It is fascinating that Lastheneia's home – Mantinea – is the provenance attributed to Diotima (*Symp.* 201d5). The connection between these two women is intriguing but mysterious. If Diotima was indeed Plato's invention, it is possible that his student Lastheneia may have been his inspiration for this character. On the other hand, if Plato's Diotima was based on a historical figure from Mantinea, it is possible that she may have been a female relative or teacher of Lastheneia which might indicate the presence of female-to-female

---

[61] Plato admired Pythagoras and the Pythagorean way of life: *Resp.* X, 600b. On the ancient tradition associating Plato's travels to Sicily with his acquisition of Pythagorean writings, see Riginos 1976: 169–174.

[62] *Phd.* 57a-59c; Riedwig 2002: 113.

[63] *Phd.* 57a7-8; Aristoxenus, fr. 11 in D.L. 8.4 (which lists the last Pythagoreans nine or ten generations after Pythagoras, including several from Phlius such as Echecrates). Iamblichus (*VP* 267) lists four male Pythagoreans from Phlius, including Echecrates, and one Pythagorean woman, Echecrateia. Zhmud 2012: 116, notes the *Catalogue* is organised by *poleis* where there were Pythagorean societies.

[64] Nails 2002: 138; Riedwig, 2002: 105–106, 136; Zhmud 2012: 107.

[65] Zhmud 2012: 63–64, argues that Aristoxenus lived in or visited Phlius before he went to Athens to study under Xenophilus and Aristotle.

philosophical transmission between Platonist women. However, these possible links between Diotima and Lastheneia are speculative.

2.3 Conclusion

Overall, women philosophers feature significantly in the world of Plato, though they were in a minority. It is significant that Plato's Socrates claims that he was taught by two women – Diotima and Aspasia – since he rarely mentions his own teachers in Plato's corpus. The only other teacher Plato's Socrates mentions is Connus (*Menex.* 235e9-236a1; *Euthyd.* 272c2-5).[66] Thus, women make up the majority (two-thirds) of Socrates' teachers named by Plato. Since Plato consistently associates Socrates with women as his teachers, Elena Duvergès Blair has argued convincingly that Plato took his approach towards the equality of women from the historical Socrates (Blair 1996: 345–348). Whether or not this is the case, Plato's emphasis on Socrates' respect for – and learning from – women suggests that the latter's approach towards women is significant for philosophical development and practice. This is particularly supported by Diotima's teaching, one of the most important speeches in Plato's works which is constitutive in defining what 'the philosopher' and 'philosophy' is, for Plato. Diotima's speech – when taken in tandem with Socrates' approach to the Pythia's Oracle and the woman in his dream – suggests that the content of women's teaching of Socrates is often oracular, mystical or religious (Blair 1996: 335) and that this dimension of wisdom is important, even central, to philosophy (see Section 5).

Women were also pupils in Plato's Academy and played an active role in this philosophical setting, although we know little about their intellectual activities.[67] These women may have been attracted to Plato's philosophy and inspired to study with him because of his account of women and their capacity for philosophy in the *Republic*; the latter may have resonated with later generations of Platonist women philosophers as well. Since Plato's female students became well-known in antiquity, they almost certainly acted as philosophical role-models for subsequent generations of women who engaged with Plato's philosophy.

It is significant that both women who feature in Plato's works and his female students are all said to be foreigners: non-Athenian women from other regions

---

[66] At *Resp.* 400b1, c5, Socrates mentions Damon as an authority on music to be consulted but does not claim that Damon was his personal teacher.

[67] In the absence of such testimony, Reeve (2001) has written several philosophical dialogues which feature Lastheneia and Axiothea as interlocutors discussing a range of themes from Plato's *Republic* (including women, art, justice and Forms); this work is useful for educational purposes.

of Greece and Ionia. This may reflect greater access to education for women in areas of the Greek world beyond Athens, as well as possibly indicating links between Platonist and Pythagorean circles. The evidence indicates that some women, like men, travelled a great distance to study philosophy with Plato, But in terms of female agency, it also reflects the courage and independence of mind of these women – counted as 'outsiders' in Athens – in engaging in philosophical practice in a male-dominated and patriarchal environment. Indeed, their response to the marginalisation they faced – not only as women but as foreigners or metics – may well have assisted in the cultivation of qualities considered crucial for philosophical practice, such as open-mindedness, self-sufficiency, cosmic consciousness and a willingness to think beyond and question conventional, and especially binary, categories and frameworks.

3 Women in Later Platonism

In later Platonism, women played significant roles as philosophers, teachers, patrons, students and ethical role models. The flourishing of women in these roles was partially facilitated by their greater access to education during the Roman imperial period and late antiquity. While wealth and social status remained far more important prerequisites in terms of gaining literacy and writing skills for women than for men, we have evidence that girls and women had more access to education from the Hellenistic period onwards (Bagnall & Cribiore 2015: 48). Subsidised education was introduced in many cities: epigraphic evidence demonstrates that girls benefitted from these local schools, for example at Teos and Pergamon (Cole 1981). The Middle Platonist Plutarch and the majority of Neoplatonist philosophers encouraged the participation of women in their philosophical schools and communities.

3.1 Women in Middle Platonism

The greater emphasis on female education from the Hellenistic period onwards undoubtedly affected the women associated with Middle Platonism, who were literate and well-educated. The evidence for women's engagement in Middle Platonism comes from Plutarch of Chaeronea, a Platonist philosopher who was a polymath, biographer, statesman, and priest of Apollo at Delphi (see Section 5.2). After studying at the Platonist Ammonius' school in Athens,[68] Plutarch directed his own small, informal private Platonic school at home where he taught a group of young and more mature students. They read Platonic texts and had philosophical discussions, as well as reading works authored by

---

[68] Plutarch, *On the E at Delphi* 391e; Russell 1973: 4–5; von Wilamowitz-Moellendorf 1995: 49; Roskam 2021: 5–7.

philosophers associated with other philosophical schools, such as Epicurean treatises.[69] Plutarch had an extensive network of aristocratic friends from Chaeronea, Delphi, Athens and other Greek cities (Roskam 2021: 10–13). The women involved in this network possessed much philosophical and literary culture (Russell 1973: 6). Plutarch discussed philosophy and tried to live a philosophical way of life with his wife Timoxena, but also had at least one female student, Eurydice, and addresses two works to a woman called Clea, a relative of Eurydice.

3.1.1 Clea and Eurydice

Clea was the leader of the Dionysian *thyias*, a 'sacred group' of female devotees of Dionysus at Delphi.[70] She was active in the Isis cult, in which she had been initiated as a child.[71] Clea was Plutarch's philosophical colleague and is the dedicatee and addressee of his treatises *On Isis and Osiris* and *Virtues in Women*. Although she does not speak directly in these works (as Plutarch's male interlocutors usually do), Plutarch frequently addresses her directly and treats her as a philosopher. He alludes to her literacy and philosophical *paideia*, mentioning her familiarity with a wide range of books (*Virtues in Women* 243d) and philosophical conversations with her (242e). The philosophical sophistication of the two treatises (and Plutarch's explicit statements therein) attest to Clea's philosophical skill.[72] Plutarch reports that the treatise *Virtues in Women* was requested by Clea and resulted from their lengthy philosophical conversation (242 f). It is significant that Clea acted as a catalyst for the writing of this work (see Section 4.2).

Clea's relative Eurydice (Roman name: Memmia Eurydice) was one of Plutarch's philosophy students. Both women are attested in epigraphic evidence from Delphi (see Section 5.2). Plutarch dedicates his treatise *Advice to the Bride and Groom* to Eurydice and her husband Pollianus, offering this work as a wedding gift (*Advice* 138c20-21).[73] He gives advice on cultivating a harmonious marriage to the couple, claiming that philosophy helps couples to be gentle and amenable to each other and reminding them that they have often heard the main points of this teaching when they were his students (138b-c). While Plutarch offers individual advice to Eurydice and Pollianus, this sometimes differs considerably and indicates Plutarch's traditional view that the wife

---

[69] Russell 1973: 13; Roskam 2021: 9.
[70] Plutarch, *On Isis and Osiris* 364e2-4; Pomeroy 1999: 42. On Clea as a philosopher-priestess, see Section 5.2.
[71] *On Isis and Osiris* 364e2-6; 351e9-f2, 352c2-8; Stadter 1999: 173.
[72] *On Isis and Osiris* 351e6-f2, 354b13-c6, 354f9-13, 370d2-371a5, 373e7-f5; Stadter 1999: 173.
[73] On the identity of Pollianus, see Pomeroy 1999: 42–43; Puech 1992.

should subordinate herself to her husband (139 c-e, 140a, 140d, 143 f). In the closing section, Plutarch addresses Eurydice and Pollianus individually but concludes by advising Eurydice to have splendid thoughts of herself since she shares in the fruits of the Muses: education and philosophy (146a). He exhorts her to read and memorise 'what Timoxena wrote to Aristylla about the love of ornament' (145a7-9).[74] This is perhaps the only time in the surviving evidence that a male Platonist philosopher encourages a female student to learn from other another woman's writing. As such, the exhortation may attest to female-to-female transmission of philosophical ideas and advice among Middle Platonist women.

3.1.2 Timoxena

We also hear about Timoxena in Plutarch's *Consolation to his wife*, a philosophical letter where Plutarch comforts his wife after the death of their two-year old daughter (also called Timoxena) because he was away on political business when she died (*Consolation* I, 608b1-4).[75] Letters of consolation, designed to comfort the bereaved and reflect in philosophical terms on the nature of death, were an important element of philosophical practice in the Roman period. Plutarch had almost certainly read letters of condolence authored by Cicero, Servius Sulpicius Rufus, Seneca the Younger and others, and a *Consolation to Apollonius* is preserved among his works (Pomeroy 1999: 77). Similar letters of consolation (usually authored by the educated elite) are also found among the papyri from Roman Egypt (Pomeroy 1999: 77). The 'letter of consolation' was an established literary genre with its own conventions; however, this does not diminish the genuine character of Plutarch's words since 'Greeks and Romans normally confronted rites of passage with traditional, ritualized behaviour' (Pomeroy 1999: 77). The letter is intended to be therapeutic for Plutarch and Timoxena, helping them to come to terms with their grief through philosophical reflection on the nature of death. It may have been intended for a wider audience, though this is uncertain (Pomeroy 1999: 76). If so, it was probably aimed at women specifically.

Within this letter, Plutarch characterises Timoxena as a virtuous woman, a paragon of moderation. Plutarch's depiction may reflect his attempt to present his wife as the ideal wife as formulated within his *Advice to the Bride and Groom*.[76] Nevertheless, when combined with what we know about her letter to

---

[74] On Timoxena's letter, see Section 4.1.1.
[75] On the circumstances in which Plutarch wrote this letter, see Pomeroy 1999: 75–76. This letter is dated to ca. 85-95 CE: see Jones 1966.
[76] Hawley 1999: 125–127; Pomeroy 1999: 76; Roskam 2021: 8–9.

Aristylla which contained moral advice, Timoxena seems to have been an empowering role model to contemporary women interested in philosophy. Plutarch's letter has a personal, affectionate and genuine tone, containing several hints that Plutarch and Timoxena practised philosophy together and tried to adhere to its ethical guidelines in their daily lives (Addey 2017: 420). Much of the advice in the letter relates to moral conduct in grief (*Consolation* 2, 608b10-c3). It specifically refers to philosophical ideas in a way which indicates Timoxena's understanding of a range of philosophic theories associated with several philosophical schools, but especially Plato's philosophy. This includes philosophical ideas about the nature of the soul and eschatological theories drawn from Plato and Epicureanism, as well as the idea that happiness depends on right thinking, which results in a stable frame of mind (*Consolation* 9, 611a4-5; 10, 611d-e).[77]

3.2 Women in Neoplatonism

In late antiquity, we find women who were teachers or students in almost every Neoplatonic philosophical school, including Plotinus' school in Rome, Iamblichus' school in Syria, and in the Athenian and Alexandrian schools. The location of Neoplatonic schools across the Mediterranean – in Rome, Greece, Syria, Asia Minor and Egypt – entails a diverse range of educational contexts, since women's access to education varied according to geographic region. Neoplatonic schools had extensive links with each other, with members often studying in one school and teaching in another. Frequently, male philosophers associated with these schools would arrange for their daughters or female relatives to marry a male philosopher associated with another Neoplatonic school: familial links connected these communities. Neoplatonist philosophers tended to encourage women's participation in philosophy. As well as drawing on Plato, they were likely influenced by Plutarch's approach towards the inclusion of women in philosophy.[78]

3.2.1 Female Teachers in Neoplatonism

Three Neoplatonic women philosophers are presented as teachers in the extant ancient sources: Sosipatra of Ephesus, Hypatia of Alexandria and Asclepigeneia of Athens. Sosipatra and Hypatia also became the Heads of philosophical schools, an unusual attainment for women in antiquity. Since

---

[77] See Addey 2017: 420–421.
[78] Photius, *Bibliotheca* 161 reports that he had seen a work of Sopater (Iamblichus' pupil) and that vols. 8-11 contained extracts from Plutarch: see Sandbach 1969: 2.

Sosipatra likely acted as a role model for – and influenced – Asclepigeneia, it is worth examining these women alongside each other.

Sosipatra and Asclepigeneia

Sosipatra (early-mid fourth century CE) and Asclepigeneia the Elder (late fourth to early fifth centuries CE), who are presented as philosophers, teachers and theurgists, are each only attested in one source: Eunapius' *Lives of the Philosophers and Sophists* (*Vitae Sophistarum*), which associates Sosipatra with Iamblichus' philosophic successors, and Marinus' *Proclus, Or on Happiness*, which presents Asclepigeneia as the theurgic teacher of Proclus, the main biographical subject of the work (*Proc.* 28).[79] She was the daughter of Plutarch of Athens, who was Head of the Athenian School in the late fourth and early fifth centuries CE (*Proc.* 28.12-13).[80] In Section 5.3, I examine their roles as theurgists and philosopher-priestess figures; here we focus on their teaching activities within Neoplatonic schools.

Sosipatra chose to marry Eustathius, a pupil of Iamblichus, and eventually became Head of the Neoplatonic School at Pergamon alongside Aedesius, one of Iamblichus' main successors (*VS* 6.9.1.1-6). The chronology surrounding her life and that of Eustathius is complex but she was almost certainly active in the 330s and 340s CE (Penella 1990: 53–56). Although Sosipatra is only attested in Eunapius, we can be certain of her historicity given her connections with prominent late antique figures, including Eustathius, Maximus of Ephesus and her son Antoninus.[81] Eunapius was taught by Chrysanthius of Sardis, who had been a pupil of Aedesius and Sosipatra, and so offers an 'insider' account of these figures (Watts 2017: 97). On this basis, Edward Watts (2005) has argued that it is useful to see Eunapius' work as a form of 'oral history'. With regard to Asclepigeneia, we might treat Marinus' work as 'oral history' as well (while remaining cognisant of its hagiographical features), since he was the pupil and successor of Proclus, a direct eyewitness to and 'insider' of the Athenian School.

Sosipatra is the only woman who receives a biography in Eunapius' work (*VS* 6.6.5-6.9.17), although her inclusion is qualified:

> 'So far did the fame of this woman travel that it is fitting for me to speak of her at greater length, even in this catalogue of wise men' (*VS* 6.6.6.1-3, trans. Wright 1921).

---

[79] The date of Eunapius' work is uncertain but it was composed 396–405 CE: see Penella 1990: 9–23. Asclepigeneia may be the unnamed 'Athenian woman' mentioned by Damascius: see Section 5.3.

[80] Asclepigeneia's descendants: see Marinus, *Proc.* 12.30-31, 29.5-31.

[81] On Sosipatra's historicity, see Johnston 2012: 100, n.8.

Eunapius issues an implicit apology for his focus on Sosipatra, a move which may reflect his own patriarchal assumptions about the capacities of women or that of his (mostly male) readership. His statement indicates that the male philosopher or sage was seen as the standard subject for late antique *Lives*, which accords with the wider pattern evident in our sources (see Section 1.2). Sosipatra, like her contemporary Hypatia, was unusual in receiving such detailed treatment, indicating that both women were exceptionally talented. Eunapius notes that Sosipatra was intellectually and spiritually gifted, surpassing many of the men around her (*VS* 6.6.5.1-6.1; 6.7.5.1-3).

Sosipatra had an unconventional education: she was taught by two 'Chaldean' strangers who turned up at her father's house when she was five years old and educated her for the next five years (*VS* 6.6.7.1-6.7.2.1). When they leave, these 'Chaldeans' entrusted Sosipatra with ritual tools and books in a chest for safekeeping: this demonstrates that they had trained her in ritual practices (6.7.8.2-9.1). One of the functions of Eunapius' account is to portray Sosipatra as a Chaldean initiate in order to link Iamblichus' philosophic community to the Chaldean Oracles through her (Addey 2018: 148–149).

Eunapius does not give much information about Sosipatra's teaching practices in the School at Pergamon; as with his male subjects, he focuses on the way that she exemplifies the holy life, which he identifies with theurgy (Schultz 2023: 197). He emphasises Sosipatra's unusual 'psychic' abilities and oracular visions (see Section 5.3).[82] However, when reporting one of her visions which occurred while teaching, he states:

> Once, for example, when they all met at her house ... the theme under discussion and their inquiry was concerning the soul. Several theories were propounded, and then Sosipatra began to speak, and gradually by her proofs disposed of their arguments; then she fell to discoursing on the descent of the soul, and what part of it is subject to punishment, what part immortal ... (*VS* 6.9.11.1-12.4)

Sosipatra responded to her students' comments and questions relating to different theories concerning the nature of the soul, using proofs to refute some of these arguments. Sosipatra was likely discussing Plato's *Republic* X, especially the 'Myth of Er' which focuses on the descent of the soul, with her students (Marx 2021: 81). Additionally, she may have discussed the arguments for the immortality of the soul in Plato's *Phaedo*, given that this was the third dialogue in Iamblichus' teaching curriculum, which systematised Plato's dialogues into a specific order for pedagogical purposes. Sosipatra and Asclepigeneia taught an inner circle of students within their homes and largely focused on advanced

---

[82] Denzey-Lewis 2014: 276–277; Addey 2018.

subjects such as theurgy and religious mysteries (Watts 2017: 98–101). Yet this passage demonstrates that Sosipatra also taught subjects that were part of the standard Neoplatonist curriculum, since she is depicted as teaching traditional Platonic themes: the nature, immortality and descent of the soul (Marx 2021: 73, 85–89). This passage indicates that dialectic and dialogue were important aspects of her teaching methods, which may reflect Diotima's use of philosophical elenchus and dialogue in teaching Socrates (Plato, *Symp.* 201e3-4).[83] Although Neoplatonists often produced commentaries rather than dialogues, the use of elenchus, inherited from Plato's Socrates, was important in their teaching methods within the context of their extensive use of dialogic questioning and answering in the classroom.[84]

Asclepigeneia was the daughter of a well-respected philosopher, Plutarch of Athens, who supervised her education, although we hear nothing about her training. She became Proclus' teacher of theurgy, the latter of whom succeeded Plutarch of Athens and Syrianus as Head of the Athenian School in 437 CE. Therefore, Asclepigeneia was teaching in the early 430s CE (after Proclus joined the school in 429/30 CE) and may have taught other advanced students prior to this. She seemingly taught in the household of her father which was part of the Athenian School since Plutarch also taught his most advanced students there, including Proclus, who studied Aristotle's *On the Soul* and Plato's *Phaedo* with Plutarch at the same time or soon after he took lower-level classes with Syrianus (*Proc.* 12).[85] Like Sosipatra, Asclepigeneia taught in a domestic environment; many Neoplatonic schools were based in the private household of a philosopher or patron.

Like Sosipatra, Asclepigeneia must have been an extremely proficient philosopher in order to become a teacher of theurgy (Watts 2017: 100), since the practice of theurgy presupposes the study of philosophy both prior to and in tandem with ritual practice (Addey 2017: 428–429). Yet we hear little about Asclepigeneia's philosophical skills, since Marinus only mentions her briefly when describing Proclus' theurgic virtue. It is reasonable to assume that Asclepigeneia would have been familiar with Plato's *Republic*, since Proclus wrote a commentary on this work.[86] Since this work was known in the Athenian School, Asclepigeneia's father, Plutarch of Athens, would have ensured her familiarity with it and Asclepigeneia may have been inspired in her philosophical studies and teaching by Plato's account of women in the *Republic*. Like her

---

[83] Addey 2018: 155, 2024: 470.
[84] See Porphyry, *Plot.* 13, on Plotinus' teaching methods; Eunapius, *VS* 5.3.4.1-3, on Iamblichus.
[85] On the teaching structures and locations of the Athenian School, see Watts 2017: 52–54, 100.
[86] On Proclus' interpretation of Plato's account of women in the *Republic*, see Adamson 2023: 232–238.

predecessor Sosipatra, Asclepigeneia taught a select group of advanced students, since theurgy was seen as the culmination of philosophy within the Athenian School and 'theurgic virtue' was considered the peak in the attainment of the six virtues evident in Proclus' own philosophic range of achievements depicted by Marinus (Watts 2017: 100). We have no evidence that Asclepigeneia taught philosophy to less advanced students but, as with Sosipatra, we should not dismiss this possibility.

Hypatia of Alexandria

Hypatia of Alexandria (ca. 355–415 CE) is the most famous woman philosopher examined in this Element. She was the daughter of the mathematician Theon and became a well-respected philosopher, teacher and political advisor, eventually becoming Head of Theon's School. Several sources mention her, focusing mostly on her murder by Christian monks in Alexandria in 415 CE. While her murder was related to the political conflict between Orestes, the governor of Alexandria, and Cyril, the Christian bishop and to the wider religious conflict between pagans and Christians in Alexandria at the time, Gillian Clark has noted 'both the content and fact of her teaching no doubt contributed to her being lynched by a Christian mob' (Clark 1993: 133). Indeed, this violence serves as a reminder that women philosophers faced dangerous obstacles in teaching philosophy publicly. Hypatia has been the subject of numerous works over the centuries and several fictional accounts have been influential; she is even the main protagonist of a film *Agora* (2004). Many of these works are imbued with legend and her image has been distorted by ideological biases: for example, in European literature of the Enlightenment period, she was often used as an instrument in religious and philosophical polemic.[87]

We know little about Hypatia's education, but she likely moved directly from home language instruction under a tutor into Theon's school, possibly undertaking grammatical training in a class with other girls and boys under the supervision of one of Theon's teaching assistants (Watts 2017: 26–27). After this, Hypatia was taught mathematics and possibly philosophy by her father in her late teens or early twenties (Watts 2017: 27). Damascius' account of Hypatia (*Phil. Hist* fr. 43A-E) emphasises her moral virtues rather than her intellectual achievements, but reports that she ' ... was endowed with a nobler nature than her father, she was not content with the mathematical education that her father gave her, but occupied herself with some distinction in the other branches of philosophy' (fr. 43A, l.2-4). He presents Hypatia as far more talented than her

---

[87] On the reception of Hypatia, see Dzielska 1995: 1–26; Watts 2017: 135–147.

father and also suggests that she re-calibrated the balance between mathematics and philosophy, asserting the greater importance of philosophy but adhering to mathematical training as important preparation for philosophical study, as it had been since Plato's time.[88] At some point, Hypatia moved from being a student in her father's school to being one of his colleagues; she became a well-respected teacher in Alexandria (Watts 2017: 29). Theon turned the role of primary instructor over to Hypatia in the early or mid-380s and she probably became the effective head of the School in the same decade (while Theon was still the official head) and nominal head of the school in the 390s.[89] From the letters of Synesius, a pupil of Hypatia, we know that her students were male, some Christian and some pagan, and many later held imperial or ecclesiastical positions (Dzielska 1995: 37–38).

Hypatia taught the philosophy of Plato, Aristotle and other philosophers in a public setting (Damascius, *Phil. Hist.* fr. 43A, l.4-7). Her teaching included mathematics and astronomy, as well as the reading and discussion of canonical philosophical texts and study of the more recent interpretive traditions surrounding them (Watts 2017: 31). Hypatia is the only Neoplatonist woman philosopher firmly credited with writing philosophical works; her writings focused heavily on mathematics and astronomy (see Section 4.1.1). There is much debate about the kind of philosophy that Hypatia taught: partly on the basis of Socrates Scholasticus' testimony, some argue that she taught philosophy in the tradition of Plotinus and Porphyry.[90] Others postulate that she was engaged in theurgy, although this is contested (see Section 5). Damascius describes Hypatia as a gifted teacher who used the method of dialectic in her teaching and philosophical investigation (fr. 43A, 7-9, 43E, 2) and that she acted as a political advisor to officials in Alexandria (fr. 43E, 1-5), which points to an interest in political philosophy, as well as ethics (Schultz 2023: 203).

Hypatia has sometimes been seen as an anomalous exception, a kind of 'token woman' in the history of women philosophers. Yet she was part of a wider network and had several female contemporaries: as well as the Neoplatonic philosophers, Sosipatra and Asclepigeneia, Hypatia has similarities with Pandrosion, an early fourth-century Alexandrian female mathematician, who also taught male students in a public setting and is known from Pappas' arguments against her in his *Collectio*, which suggests that she was a younger rival of his and a contemporary of Theon, whom the young Hypatia

---

[88] On the broader intellectual context in Alexandria, see Watts 2017: 31–35.
[89] Dzielska 1995: 27; Watts 2017: 38–39.
[90] Socrates Scholasticus, *Historia Ecclesiastica* 7.14 in LaValle Norman & Petkas 2020: 249; Watts 2017: 42–46; Geertz 2020: 133–150.

would have known about.[91] Hypatia was exceptionally talented, her combination of intellectual achievements are unusual and she attained a high level of independence in teaching publicly and acting as a political advisor. In her public activities, Hypatia was probably influenced by earlier Egyptian social conditions. In Dynastic Egypt, women had an unusual degree of freedom and were considered equal to men in legal and social terms. Although these rights to equal status were gradually eroded in the Ptolemaic and Roman periods (Tyldesley 1994: 44), they likely had a long-lasting effect on women living in Egypt even in these milieux. A woman as learned as Hypatia would have been familiar with the history of social conditions for women in Egypt.

3.2.2 Female Students and Patrons in Neoplatonism

Plotinus' School in Rome (which operated from approximately 246 to 268/269 CE) is presented by Porphyry as an inclusive environment: anyone who wished could attend his lectures and meetings (*Plot.* 1.13-15). This included women, who were a catalytic and central part of this philosophical community: Plotinus' school was based in the household of Gemina the Elder, who was a devoted student (*Plot.* 9.1-2).[92] Gemina was a significant catalyst for Plotinus' philosophical teaching since, as patron, she provided him with the venue and resources necessary to establish his school and foster his philosophical community. She presumably influenced the character and environment of the school: many of Plotinus' friends (male and female) entrusted him with guardianship of their children (*Plot.* 9.5-10). Another woman, Chione, also lived in the household (*Plot.* 11.2-8). Plotinus' school was a community full of widows and children, a women – and child-friendly community.[93] The roles of women as patrons and supporters of Neoplatonic philosophical schools is important and corresponds with the wider rise of women (especially aristocratic widows) acting as patrons of philosophy and the arts in the Roman period and especially as patrons of early Christianity. Diogenes Laertius had an unnamed female patron who financially supported his work and loved Plato: her familiarity with Plato is the main reason for his brief treatment of Platonic doctrine (D.L. 3.47). It is unclear if she was a fully fledged philosopher or an aristocratic woman with intellectual interests but she had read Plato's works extensively (Long 2018: xxiii).

Plotinus held public lectures open to visitors and informal members, and more sustained philosophical sessions with the 'inner circle' of his devoted

---

[91] On Pandrosion and Hypatia, see Watts 2017: 94–97.
[92] Gemina was aristocratic; on her possible identity, see Hadot 1993: 91; O'Meara 2003: 14.
[93] Hadot 1993: 91; Wilberding 2022: 60–61.

followers (*Plot.* 7.1-2; 13-15), Of the fourteen regular, dedicated members of Plotinus' school, three were women: Gemina the Elder, her daughter, Gemina the Younger, and Amphiclea, who became the wife of Ariston, Iamblichus' son. Porphyry reports that all three women had a great devotion to philosophy, making it clear that they were part of Plotinus' inner circle (*Plot.* 9.1-6). As devoted members, these women must have participated in philosophical sessions with Plotinus, including reading and discussing Plato's works and those of Severus, Gaius, Atticus, Numenius, Cronius, Alexander of Aphrodisias, Adrastus and Aspasius (*Plot.* 14.10-17). Although difficult to ascertain, it is likely that these women were bilingual since knowledge of Greek would have been important to understanding the works read out in Plotinus' sessions; these women lived in Rome and must have spoken Latin too.

Porphyry follows Plotinus in facilitating women's involvement in philosophy: a philosophical letter survives which he wrote to his wife Marcella (whom he married late in life after her husband, Porphyry's friend, died), the content of which demonstrates that Porphyry practised philosophy with her. The letter is protreptic, encouraging Marcella to be self-sufficient in pursuing philosophy while he is away (*Marc.* 4.58-59), but may have been intended for publication to encourage women (especially widows like Marcella) to pursue philosophy.[94] Porphyry describes Marcella's natural aptitude for philosophy and their shared philosophical way of life (3.36-38, 44-46). He presents philosophy as an ascent to the gods (6.99-108, 7.131-134), discussing Plato's teaching of the intelligible and sensible when exhorting Marcella to ascend within herself to the intelligible (10.179-186). He reminds Marcella that traditional religion is part of the philosophic way of life, and the divine is present everywhere (11.191-192). He also discusses the relationship between the soul and the body, and the role of the virtues in the philosophic life in a Platonic manner (10.183-86). A wide range of Neoplatonic metaphysical notions are evident in the letter. Damascius refers to Porphyry's wife as the 'holy Marcella', suggesting her elevated status in later Neoplatonic circles (*Phil. Hist.* fr. 49, 1-2). We know little about Marcella's identity; she may possibly have been the daughter of Marcellus Orontius, a student of Plotinus (*Plot.* 7.29-32).

Female Students in Iamblichus' School

At least three factors suggest that there were female students in Iamblichus' school in Apamea, Syria, although the evidence is circumstantial. First, Iamblichus was deeply influenced by Pythagoreanism, including the prominence of women in Pythagorean communities. As discussed, Iamblichus includes

---

[94] Whittaker 2001: 150–168; Brisson 2022: 64.

seventeen Pythagorean women in his *Catalogue* of Pythagoreans (*VP* 267). Secondly, Iamblichus addresses one of his philosophical letters to a woman called Arete, who may have been his student. Third, his philosophic successor, Aedesius, moved the location of Iamblichus' school to Pergamon after his death and taught there alongside Sosipatra. The prominent role of Sosipatra in the School at Pergamon suggests the openness of Iamblichus' philosophical community to women.

Iamblichus addresses one of his philosophical letters on the topic of 'self-control' (σωφροσύνη) to Arete.[95] She is likely identical with the Arete mentioned by Emperor Julian, who travelled to Phrygia in person to assist her in resolving problems with her neighbours (*Letter to Themistius* 259d). While the identification is uncertain, the way in which Julian speaks of her with great respect, referring to her as 'that wonderful woman' (ἡ θαθμασία), indicates her respected status within Neoplatonic circles.[96] The dating of Julian's visit to Arete is unknown but probably occurred in the 350s, when Arete would have been quite an old woman; she may have moved to Phrygia from Syria in the wake of Aedesius' moving of the School to Pergamon (Dillon & Polleichtner 2009: xviii, n.8).

Whether Arete was a member of Iamblichus' school is uncertain but very likely since many of Iamblichus' letters are addressed to his own pupils.[97] These letters survive only in fragmentary form, but of the twenty extant letters, nine are addressed to individuals who were definitely his pupils (Dexippus, Eustathius and Sopater), and one is addressed to Anatolius, almost certainly Iamblichus' old teacher (Dillon & Polleichtner 2009: xvii–xix). Arete was educated and well-read in the classics of philosophy and literature, such that she could appreciate the numerous references in Iamblichus' letter (Dillon & Polleichtner 2009: 62). These include direct citations of the *Phaedo* (83d) and *Phaedrus* (253b), showing that Arete had knowledge of a range of Plato's dialogues (Letter 3, fr. 2). Iamblichus discusses the range of influence of self-control as a virtue, defining it as an 'orderliness' (εὐκοσμία) between the three parts or 'powers' of the soul: reason (λόγος), spiritedness (θυμός) and the appetitive part (ἐπιθυμία), referring to the tripartite nature of the soul set out in Plato's *Republic* IV (fr. 1). The power of self-control is extended to the whole cosmos as the harmoniser of the elements and seasons, broadening the scope of

---

[95] *Letter 3: To Arete*; ed. Dillon & Polleichtner 2009: 62.
[96] Dillon & Polleichtner 2009: xviii with n.8, 62; Addey 2017: 423–424. Julian's comment at 267d-268a may allude to Arete, one of only two people mentioned in the letter whom Julian says that he assisted in times of danger, further strengthening the likelihood of Arete being a philosopher.
[97] These include Letters 3, 7 and 12: see Dillon and Polleichtner 2009; Denzey-Lewis 2014: 279; Addey 2017: 425.

the letter to include cosmology as well as ethics (fr. 7). Iamblichus refers to allegorical interpretations of two traditional Greek myths (fr. 3 and 4); the use of allegory was widespread among Neoplatonists and suggests Arete's status as a philosopher or student of philosophy.

Significantly, fragments 2 and 3 of the letter allude to the 'purificatory' level of virtue in accordance with the Neoplatonic schema of the virtues established by Plotinus and developed by Porphyry, since they discuss the 'elimination' of desires (ἀπάθεια, associated with purificatory virtue), rather than their 'moderation' (μετριοπάθεια, associated with the lower level of political/civic virtue).[98] Since purificatory virtue was considered superior to civic virtue by Neoplatonists because it was held to free the soul from the body and, consequently, to lead more directly to the goal of becoming like a god than civic virtue (considered to enable us to control our lower souls and so contributes towards divinisation in a preparatory sense), Iamblichus would only address a philosopher, or student, in this way, indicating that Arete was either Iamblichus' student or a philosopher in her own right.[99]

Female Students in the Athenian and Alexandrian Schools

Our main evidence for teaching arrangements in the Athenian School derives from Marinus, who does not mention any female pupils although he discusses an important woman teacher: Asclepigeneia. Since she had attained such proficiency in theurgy that she could teach Proclus, she must have studied philosophy which indicates she may have been a pupil (alongside the male students) in the Athenian School, although her father, Plutarch of Athens, seemingly taught her privately at home. Since Plutarch also taught Proclus and other advanced students in his home, the boundaries between the Athenian School and the latter's household were somewhat permeable in any case (see Section 3.2.1). Damascius reports that Aedesia, the philosopher Hermeias' wife, brought her sons from Alexandria to the Athenian School to study philosophy but there is no mention of her studying within the School (*Phil. Hist.* fr. 56, 21-23). Whether she attained philosophical skills during the process does not seem to be regarded as important by Damascius (Schultz 2022: 127–128).[100]

---

[98] Dillon & Polleichtner 2009: 62–63. Political level of virtue associated with μετριοπάθεια: Plotinus, *Enn.* I.2 [19], 2.14-17, 7.17-20; Porphyry, *Sent.* 32.6-8, 29-30; Brisson 2005: 132, 809 n.106. Purificatory virtue associated with ἀπάθεια: Plotinus, *Enn.* I.2 [19], 5.3-23, 6.23-28, 7.17-19, 22-26; Porphyry, *Sent.* 32.15-18, 30-32. Porphyry and Iamblichus added further 'grades' of virtue but Iamblichus follows Plotinus and Porphyry closely in relation to the parameters of the political and purificatory levels: see Finamore 2012: 126–147.

[99] Purificatory virtue as superior to the political level: Plotinus, *Enn.* I.2 [19] 1.21-28, 3.1-3, 7.22-31; Porphyry, *Sent.* 32.29-32; Brisson 2005: 133-135; Finamore 2012: 125, 133–134.

[100] On Aedesia, see Section 5.3.3.

In relation to the Alexandrian School, we hear about some of the female pupils of Damascius and Isidore. In his summary of Damascius' *Life of Isidore* (also known as the *Philosophical History*), Photius reports that Damascius dedicated this work to Theodora, who had been his and Isidore's student along with her sisters. Theodora is described as 'a Hellene by religious persuasion, not unacquainted with the disciplines of philosophy, poetics and grammar, but also well-versed in geometry and higher arithmetic' (Damascius, *Phil. Hist.* Testimonia III = Photius, *Bibl. Cod.* 181). Photius asserts that she was the daughter of Kyrina and Diogenes, and a distant relative of Iamblichus. Theodora acted as a catalyst in convincing Damascius to write this biography of Isidore (see Section 4.2).

3.3 Conclusion

In Middle Platonism, Plutarch presents the women around him as philosophers, students and empowering role models. While male (teacher) to female (student) transmission is attested in Middle Platonism, faint traces of female to female transmission are also evident in the lives and activities of Clea, Eurydice and Timoxena. With the emergence of Neoplatonism, historical women philosophers are explicitly attested as teachers for the first time, with several women, Sosipatra and Hypatia, becoming the Heads of philosophical schools. With each of these teachers, we see a pattern of female (teacher) to male (student) philosophical transmission. There is some evidence for women as patrons of philosophical schools, while much evidence confirms the considerable number of female students associated with Neoplatonism. Even though women remained a minority, they had a significant impact on the formation, teaching practices and development of later Platonist philosophical schools and communities.

4 Female Philosophers and Philosophical Writing

It is well-known that there are no surviving philosophical works authored by Platonist female philosophers (with the possible exception(s) discussed next). While this issue is characterised by silence and absence, and possibly by the silencing of women's words, this section examines what is known about women's philosophical writings in the Platonic tradition and suggests certain trajectories for future research. One such trajectory is to suggest a shift in our methodology using feminist epistemology: it would be useful to investigate the extent to which the preservation and transmission of women's philosophical works has been affected by 'epistemic injustice' which may be present in antiquity and in later traditions of textual transmission. As a case study,

I consider the transmission of philosophical writings produced by Hypatia. I also examine the significant role that women played in catalysing the production of specific, male-authored philosophical works, using the concept of instrumental agency, which emphasises mediation and relationality, in order to draw out the significance of this catalytic role and its implications for women's roles in Platonic philosophical schools and communities.

4.1 Platonist and Neoplatonist Women's Philosophical Writings

Hypatia is the only female philosopher in the Platonic tradition firmly credited with authoring philosophical works, which raises the issue of whether she was anomalous in this regard. I will suggest that she was not, especially since Plutarch's wife Timoxena is credited with a philosophical treatise or letter. I argue that some women philosophers in the Platonic tradition – at least from the Roman imperial period onwards in Middle Platonic and Neoplatonic contexts – *did* write philosophical works, even if these writings were not necessarily preserved or transmitted in their contemporary milieu or later centuries.

4.1.1 Hypatia of Alexandria

Hypatia ' ... wrote a *Commentary on Diophantus*, the *Astronomical Canon*, [and a] *Commentary on Apollonius' Conic Sections*' (*Suda*, s.v. Hypatia, 1. 3-5: ἔγραψεν ὑπόμνημα εἰς Διόφαντον, τὸν ἀστρονομικὸν Κανόνα, εἰς τὰ Κωνικὰ Ἀπολλωνίου ὑπόμνημα). That is, Hypatia wrote commentaries on the *Arithmetica* of Diophantus of Alexandria (second or third century CE) and on Apollonius of Perge's *Conic Sections* (third century BCE) and wrote on the astronomical canon. Many scholars have followed Paul Tannery's emendation of the entry (inserting εἰς 'on' before the title of this work) and thus construed this work as a '<Commentary on> *the Astronomical Canon*'.[101] This might refer to a commentary on Ptolemy's *Handy Tables* (πρόχειροι κανόνες τῆς ἀστρονομίας).[102] However, the word 'commentary' is not given for the *Astronomical Canon* in the Suda entry, whereas it is explicitly given for the other two works. This suggests that the middle entry is just the title of her book: *Astronomical Canon* (Cameron & Long 1993: 44–45).

The *Handy Tables* do not survive in Ptolemy's original edition but in a version widely attributed to Theon, Hypatia's father. However, the attribution is not attested in any manuscript; nor does Theon himself refer to this edition in any of his commentaries (Cameron & Long 1993: 45). On this basis, and because Theon interprets Ptolemy's own calculations in an improbable way

---
[101] Deakin 1994: 238–239; Lavalle Norman & Petkas 2020: 3. Cf. Cameron & Long 1993: 44.
[102] Rist 1965: 216; Neugebauer 1975: 838.

that suggests he did not check the figures, Alan Cameron has argued that we can infer it was Hypatia who edited this text.[103] Further support for this interpretation comes from the sub-title to Book 3 of Theon's *Commentary on the Almagest*:

> Commentary by Theon of Alexandria on the third book of Ptolemy's *Almagest*, edition (ἐκδοσεως) revised by my daughter, the philosopher Hypatia (Theon, *Commentary on the Almagest* III).[104]

It has been assumed that it was Theon's *Commentary* that Hypatia revised.[105] Yet a major issue with this interpretation is the use of the Greek term ἔκδοσις, which refers to an 'edition', 'publication' or 'translation' rather than 'commentary'.[106] The sub-headings for Books 1 and 2 of Theon's *Commentary*, which do not mention Hypatia, suggest the solution:

> Commentary by Theon of Alexandria on his own edition (τῆς παρ' αὐτοῦ γεγενημένης ἐκδοσεως) of the first (second) book of Ptolemy's *Almagest* (*Commentary on the Almagest* I, II).[107]

The editor of Theon's commentary claims that this is Theon's original edition, in contrast to Hypatia's (Rome 1943: 317 n.1). However, Cameron argues that when writing Books 1 and 2, Theon had not yet written Book 3, much less seen it revised by Hypatia. Moreover, it makes no sense for Theon to speak of a commentary on his own edition (since one's books are always in one's own edition), unless the rest of the edition was edited by Hypatia.[108] Thus, we can extrapolate that the first two books of the edition of Ptolemy's *Almagest* were edited by Theon but Book 3 was edited by Hypatia: at the least, the work was produced by a collaboration between Hypatia and Theon. It is very probable that the rest of the work (Books 4–13) was edited by Hypatia, while Theon wrote the commentary on the text.[109] Hypatia collaborated with Theon in producing the

---

[103] Cameron 1990: 126–127; Cameron & Long 1993: 45.
[104] ed. Rome 1943; trans. Cameron & Long 1993.
[105] Rome 1943: cxvi–cxxi, looked in vain for linguistic differences between Book 3 of the commentary and other books.
[106] *LSJ* s.v. ἔκδοσις; s.v. ὑπόμνημα which refers to 'notes' or a 'commentary' on a published work. Cameron (1990: 112) notes that in the lexicon of the scholar, ἔκδοσις usually denotes the edition of a text, while ὑπόμνημα refers to a commentary, and this is how Theon normally used the terms.
[107] ed. Rome 1943; trans. Cameron & Long 1993.
[108] Cameron 1990: 112; Cameron & Long 1993: 46.
[109] Cameron 1990: 114–115. According to Rome 1943: II 318 n.1 (the only scholar who has looked at the MSS. for the rest of the commentary) there are no more subheadings to Books IV-XIII, which means we cannot be certain that Hypatia edited the text of these remaining books. Yet Cameron 1990: 115 notes: 'the natural assumption is that Theon found the task of both text and commentary too much for him, and persuaded Hypatia to take over the text for the rest of the project.'

edition of Ptolemy's *Almagest* – and may have actually composed the bulk of the edition – which was later attributed to Theon. As Alan Cameron concludes: 'Far from Hypatia's works being entirely lost, we may have more than 1,000 pages of Greek edited by her. The "large number of interpolations" recently detected in the *Almagest* by G.J. Toomer may be in the main Hypatia's work.'[110]

Although a contested issue, it is possible that a later Arabic translation of certain sections of Hypatia's *Commentary on Diophantus' Arithemetica* actually survives. Of the thirteen original books of Diophantus' *Arithmetica*, only six survive in Greek.[111] But we know that at least four books survived until ca. 860 CE and were translated at that point into Arabic: an Arabic manuscript contains Books 4–7 which seem to follow on from the Greek text of Books 1–3.[112] The Arabic text is an expanded version of Diophantus' text which incorporates verifications of his demonstrations, alternative resolutions, and interpolated problems. The purpose of these expansions is to make a difficult text easier to understand. Either the translator incorporated into his text material from an exegetical commentary or the text he translated had already been amplified in this way. Either way, the obvious candidate for the amplified Greek original is Hypatia, who is the only known writer in antiquity to have written a commentary on Diophantus' *Arithmetica*.[113] This raises the possibility that some of Hypatia's own writings (sections of this commentary) were transmitted via the Arabic tradition *without* attribution to her.

Was Hypatia exceptional amongst the women associated with the Platonic tradition in writing philosophical works? Is the possible attribution of some of her work to a male philosopher an exception to the rule or might it indicate a wider pattern in the tradition(s) of textual preservation and transmission? While it is difficult to prove that some of Hypatia's work was later attributed to Theon, this would accord with several extant ancient sources on Hypatia which attribute a greater level of expertise to her than her father or claim that she outshone all the philosophers of her time.[114] Likewise, the possibility that some of Hypatia's writings were preserved and transmitted in the Arabic tradition *without* attribution to her is contentious but probable.

Another case suggests that the attribution to male philosophers of works authored by ancient women did occur in the process of textual transmission. As discussed, Plutarch tells Eurydice to memorise his wife Timoxena's writing to

---

[110] Toomer 1984: 4–5, 27 n.1, 27–32; Cameron & Long 1993: 48.
[111] Cameron & Long 1993: 48; Deakin 1994: 239.
[112] Sesiano 1982; Cameron & Long 1993: 48; Addey 2022: 33.
[113] Sesiano 1982; Cameron & Long 1993: 48
[114] Damascius, *Phil. Hist.* 43A, 1-2; Socrates Scholasticus, *Historia Ecclesiastica* 7.14; Philostorgius, *Eccleasiastical History* 8.9 in Lavalle Norman & Petkas 2020: 248–249.

Aristylla on ornament (*Advice* 145a: Περὶ φιλοκοσμίας). The identity of Aristylla is unknown (Pomeroy 1999: 55). A work of the same title (Περὶ φιλοκοσμίας) is listed as one of Plutarch's works in the Lamprias Catalogue (no. 113), immediately after the *Letter of Consolation to his Wife* (no. 112). Given the apparent situation with the transmission of Hypatia's writings, it is likely that this work was incorrectly attributed to Plutarch either in late antiquity or in the medieval period when the Catalogue of Lamprias was compiled, due to mistaken (accidental) attribution or – as is more likely – because the compiler of the Catalogue doubted that a woman could have written this work (which would represent a kind of residual gender prejudice similar to epistemic injustice).[115] Almost certainly influenced by the attribution to Plutarch within the Catalogue, several scholars have argued that this letter was written by Plutarch himself rather than Timoxena.[116]

Overall, it seems that many works written by women were already – in antiquity itself – not circulated widely, not preserved or only partially preserved.[117] To publish a book in Graeco-Roman antiquity generally meant to entrust it to a circle of colleagues or students, who then undertook to ensure its circulation via copying of the manuscript and conveying it to others (Hadot 1993: 89). Because of social marginalisation as well as testimonial injustice, women's writings were less likely to be circulated and copied in antiquity. Consideration of the processes associated with textual transmission in the medieval Christian and Arabic traditions is also essential: both traditions transmitted ancient philosophical texts via the manual transcription and reproduction of manuscripts. Therefore, the survival of ancient texts relates to what was considered important in medieval Byzantium or Baghdad, and later, in the Middle Ages and Renaissance. Of course, the accidental loss of works is an important factor in textual transmission as well, since many works authored by ancient male philosophers also no longer survive. But alongside contingency, predominant views of the status and capacities of women in the medieval Christian and Arabic traditions may have affected the transmission of their writings, especially philosophical works, as Jane MacIntosh Snyder notes:

> ... during the Middle Ages and the Renaissance, philosophical inquiry became almost exclusively a male province; no doubt monks and scholars had little interest in copying or studying the works of obscure female

---

[115] On the Lamprias Catalogue, see Sandbach 1969: 3–7. The Catalogue has been found in several MSS., the oldest of which (Paris 1678) dates to the twelfth century CE. The original Catalogue may have been the inventory of a library: scholars have argued it dates to late antiquity, variously proposing dates of the third, fourth or fifth century CE.

[116] Barrow 1967, 20; von Willamowitz-Moellendorff 1995: 52 n.10. Some accept the attribution to Timoxena: Russell 1973: 6; Pomeroy 1999: 55.

[117] Snyder 1989: 100, 121; Plant 2004: 6; Addey 2022: 28–30.

philosophers, whose minds (according to the prevailing Aristotelian doctrine) would by nature have been inferior to those of their male counterparts anyway. (Snyder 1989: 100)

Medieval Christian and Arabic views of women may have influenced the transmission of texts so that certain female-authored philosophical texts were not copied or transmitted, or were sometimes transmitted anonymously (without attribution) or attributed to a male philosopher.[118] To be clear, I am not suggesting the *deliberate* suppression of women's texts by monks or scribes during textual transmission – but rather that unconscious bias, or residual prejudice, against women *affected* authorial attribution and the transmission of female-authored texts, a process affected by epistemic injustice.

4.1.2 Platonist Women and Philosophical Letters

Women are the recipients of several philosophical letters written by Middle Platonist and Neoplatonist male philosophers. Presumably some of these women were the philosophical correspondents of these philosophers and wrote letters in reply, but none of their letters survive (see Clark 1993: 134). Consequently, we only hear half of the philosophical conversation – the male half, and we do not have access to women's words directly. Given that many female-authored letters survive from the Roman period, it is likely that some women did write philosophical letters, as attested for Timoxena. Letter writing was fairly common among the aristocracy of the Mediterranean in the Roman imperial period and is attested to some extent in the Hellenistic period. More than 300 letters (preserved on papyrus or ostracon) written in Greek and Egyptian by women in Egypt (some from Alexandria) survive from the period 300 BCE to 800 CE.[119] Letters were mostly delivered informally by friends, although occasionally an official letter carrier was used (Bagnall & Cribiore 2015: 37). Letter-writing does not necessitate literacy on the part of women authors, since some were dictated to professional secretaries or scribes, although others were written directly by women (Bagnall & Cribiore 2015: 6–8, 41–46). Even when a woman used dictation to have her words recorded, this is the one genre where we see women expressing themselves on their own behalf rather than through a male who controls the representation of their thought (Bagnall & Cribiore 2015: 10).

---

[118] Christensen 2023: 188–189, discusses a fourteenth-century MS (Vatican gr. 578/II, folio 189) where the copyist states that he decided not to copy the letters written by Macrina.

[119] See Bagnall & Cribiore 2015: 1–4, 8–9, 15–17, 19, for discussion of women's letters in the Hellenistic and Roman periods.

As discussed, Plutarch wrote a *Letter of Consolation to his Wife* when their infant daughter died while he was away on business. This letter was a reply to Timoxena after she had written to inform him of their daughter's death.[120] Porphyry's *Letter to Marcella* may have been a reply to a letter written by Marcella lamenting his departure (*Marc.* 4.59-67). The Homeric allusions at the beginning of Chapter 6 suggest Porphyry refers to a letter from Marcella which alluded to Andromache's farewell speech to Hector.[121] Iamblichus wrote a philosophical letter to Arete, who may have been his student and is familiar with philosophical concepts, especially the Neoplatonic grades of virtue (see Section 3.2.2).

Some evidence attests that women associated with the Platonic tradition wrote philosophical letters or treatises. Emperor Julian corresponded with the priestess Theodora, who sent him philosophical books and letters (*Ep.* 32-34. See Section 5). As discussed, Plutarch mentions Timoxena's writing to Aristylla on ornament (*Advice* 145a). Sarah Pomeroy discusses the literary output of women like Timoxena:

> 'If this modest rate of publication is not simply an artifact of the vagaries of transmission, the reason may be that such women only had time to write one work before their literary creativity was curtailed by the demands of motherhood and wifehood' (Pomeroy 1999: 55).

Timoxena's letter seems similar to the Pythagorean letters attributed to women philosophers, some of which also focus on women's adornment and dress.[122] Like those letters, Timoxena's letter should not be dismissed as philosophically insignificant, since a well-run household and the cultivation of moderation were seen respectively as an expression of cosmic order and key to the development of the virtues (Clark 2007: 170). Moreover, male philosophers also saw household management and domestic arrangements as important subjects for philosophical analysis: Aristotle's *Politics* and Plato's *Republic* 3-4 are canonical examples (Twomey 2023: 134–151). Some, such as Plutarch and Iamblichus, also wrote philosophical letters or treatises about marriage and raising children.

4.2 Women as Catalysts for Male-authored Philosophical Writings

There is evidence from the Roman imperial period that women in Middle Platonist and Neoplatonist circles acted as catalysts who not only inspired – but actively called for – the writing of several male-authored philosophical works.[123] In doing so, these women exhibit an important kind of instrumental

---

[120] Plutarch, *Consolation* 608b; von Wilamowitz-Moellendorf 1995: 51.
[121] *Marc.* 6.94-99. See Bidez 1913: 112–113. [122] Pomeroy 1999: 55; Pellò 2022: 5–9, 29–37.
[123] For a similar case involving Marcia and the Stoic philosopher Seneca, see Langlands 2004.

agency in ensuring that specific philosophical works were written and that certain philosophical questions were explored in depth. We should not underestimate their roles and agency in catalysing these works, even if the male philosophers involved mention women's roles as catalysts only briefly.

Our first example involves the Middle Platonist Clea, the addressee and dedicatee of Plutarch's *Virtues in Women*. As Plutarch relates, it was actually Clea who caused him to write this work:

> Regarding the virtues of women, Clea, I do not hold the same opinion as Thucydides. For he declares that the best woman is she about whom there is the least talk among persons outside regarding either censure or commendation, feeling that the name of the good woman, like her person, ought to be shut up indoors and never go out. But to my mind Gorgias appears to display better taste in advising that not the form but the fame of a woman should be known to many. Best of all seems the Roman custom, which publicly renders to women, as to men, a fitting commemoration after the end of their life. So when Leontis, that most excellent woman, died, I forthwith had then a long conversation with you, which was not without some share of consolation drawn from philosophy, and now, as you desired (ὡς ἠβουλήθης), I have also written out for you the remainder of what I would have said on the topic that man's virtues and woman's virtues are one and the same. (*Virtues in Women* 242e-243a, trans. Babbit 1931)[124]

Plutarch reports the precise circumstances in which he composed this treatise: after their mutual friend Leontis died, he and Clea had a lengthy philosophical conversation about her death. We know very little about Leontis but she is attested in epigraphic evidence from Delphi (Kapetanopoulos 1966: 119–130). Clea asked Plutarch to write this work to honour the virtues of women and to argue that the virtues of men and women are the same. The crucial phrase here is 'as you desired' (ὡς ἠβουλήθης) – with these few words, Plutarch indicates that it was Clea who called for and catalysed the writing of his text. Therefore, we see Clea's active instrumental agency in at least two senses: first, we see her commitment – as well as Plutarch's – to the active memorialisation and commemoration of the achievements and moral character of women. This is made clear in their commemoration of Leontis who is described as a 'most excellent woman' (τῆς ἀρίστης), a phrase which refers to her moral character and attainment of virtue. Clea also asked Plutarch to write a work commemorating a much wider range of women and their virtues.

Secondly, Clea actively called for a work which relates to an important philosophical debate within the Platonic and Stoic traditions: whether the virtue of men and women was the same or different. This philosophical *topos* relating

---

[124] Ed. Nachstädt 1935 [1971].

to gender was instigated by Plato, who questions whether men and women have the same capacity to attain virtue and whether they attain this in the same or different kinds of activities (*Meno* 71a-73d; *Resp* V, 450 c). Plato's Socrates argues that men and women have the same capacity for virtue (*Meno* 73b4-6, 73c1-2) Late antique philosophers, such as Theodorus of Asine and Proclus, would take up and write about this topic, which by their time had become a classic issue for Platonists (Dillon 2022: 94–103). Marguerite Deslauriers (2012: 351) has argued that ancient women philosophers were not included in philosophical debates about the nature and social roles of women. However, it is clear that Clea *did* in fact participate in this important philosophical debate about women's ontological status and capacity for virtue. Plutarch's wording suggests that Clea had specifically argued for gender equality in relation to the attainment of virtue, since Plutarch says that he will write about men's and women's virtue being one and the same, indicating that Clea and Plutarch agreed with Plato.

Critics may wonder why Clea did not write a philosophical work herself on this topic: this question is largely unanswerable but we know that Clea was a priestess of Delphi, the leader of the Thyiades, and the mother of several children, so maybe she did not have time to do so. When considering ancient women philosophers, it is crucial to take into account that the experience of persistent, systematic testimonial injustice often engenders secondary harms (beyond the primary epistemic harm done to the speaker/thinker and the blockages created in the circulation of ideas and knowledge) of diminishing the thinker's confidence in their own intellectual abilities and causing considerable professional disadvantage (Fricker 2007: 46–47). In the contemporary context, testimonies of professional women show that they have actively passed their ideas to male colleagues to put forward (after experiencing epistemic injustice and mounting frustration at the incredulous reception their ideas received when presented as their own) or of allowing male colleagues to take credit for their ideas, if they express them and those ideas are subsequently only taken up when verbalised by a male colleague (Fricker 2007: 46–47). It is possible that Clea had experienced such persistent testimonial injustice within the context of philosophical discourse and thus passed on her ideas to Plutarch so that these ideas (about the equality of women and their capacity for virtue) would be well-received rather than possibly being dismissed because of testimonial injustice.

In this passage, Plutarch denigrates Thucydides' views on women (often taken as representative of the standard view of women's roles in classical Athens) while praising the Roman custom which encourages public commemorations of women. Indeed, we know that women had greater freedom and were more visible in public arenas within the Roman context. It is interesting that Plutarch praises the Roman customs relating to women here, given that he usually tends to prefer all things Greek to their Roman equivalents. Although Plutarch obtained Roman citizenship and became a statesman, he usually only uses his own and his friends' Greek (rather than Roman) names in his writings and his primary allegiance was to Greece (von Wilamowitz-Moellendorf 1995: 50–51). This suggests Clea's influence on Plutarch in relation to the formulation of his philosophical ideas about women and gender equality in relation to virtue. Plutarch certainly makes it clear that his conversation with Clea stimulated – and probably influenced – his thinking on these topics.

Our second example comes from the Neoplatonic Alexandrian School. Photius' summary of Damascius' *Life of Isidore* (composed between 517 and 526 CE; also known as the *Philosophical History*) states that Damascius dedicated this work to Theodora, who had been the student of both Damascius and Isidore, who taught her and her sisters at different times:

> Damascius dedicates Isidore's biography to her [i.e. Theodora]; it was her exhortation, together with that of certain others who joined in her request, that was responsible for the author's efforts, as he himself testifies. (Photius, *Bibl. Cod.* 181, trans. Athanassiadi 1999)[125]

Theodora called for Damascius to write the biography of Isidore to commemorate their teacher, his philosophical ideas and way of life. Photius mentions that 'others' (possibly other female students of Damascius or former students of Isidore, since we know they both taught women) joined with her request but makes it clear that it was primarily her exhortation to Damascius which catalysed the work.

Critics might object that it is problematic to see ancient women as catalysts for male-authored philosophical works: one might question whether, or to what extent, women *actively* contributed towards the work in question, and their precise role as catalysts. Even if it is conceded that women did act as catalysts for male-authored works, it might be objected that it is difficult, or impossible, to ascertain their respective intellectual contribution(s) to such works. With regard to the latter issue, this analysis has attempted to identify some methodological strategies for evaluating the roles of specific women in catalysing philosophical works. Following the approach of Rebecca Langlands, the first methodological point is that a woman's influence on a text 'may be felt particularly strongly where the male author anticipates that a specific woman may read his text, especially as an addressee or patron of that work' (Langlands 2004: 115–116). Thus, it is vital

---

[125] Damascius, *Phil. Hist.* Testimonia III, l.3-4, 8-10 = Photius, *Bibl. Cod.* 181. On Theodora, see Section 3.2.2. On the dating of Damascius' work, see Watts 2017: 125.

to pay attention to the identity of any dedicatee, addressee or patron, as well as to any programmatic statements made by the male author regarding his aims in producing the specific work. Women may influence the content and style (such as the use of specific *exempla*) of a male philosopher's work (Langlands 2004: 116–117). Therefore, it is useful to compare the content (especially the philosophical ideas and arguments) and style of any work(s) addressed or dedicated to a woman with that of other extant philosophical works (where available) authored by the same philosopher, especially when the works are comparable in terms of aims, content or genre.[126] As discussed earlier, Plutarch's assessment of the Roman approach towards women and gender, specifically the commemoration of women, differs from the approach found in his other works and suggests Clea's influence on Plutarch's thinking *and* on this aspect of the text. Additionally, when a specific philosophical topic or debate is examined in a text dedicated or addressed to a woman (such as, in the case of Plutarch and Clea, the debate about whether men and women have the same capacity for virtue), it is important to consider that specific woman as an intellectual participant and active interlocutor in that debate, utilising the concept of instrumental agency to analyse the contributions of women philosophers.

With regard to the first methodological problem outlined earlier, critics might object that even if a woman 'inspires' a male-authored text (which may be evident in the fact that the work is addressed or dedicated to her), this does not necessarily entail that she had any specific intellectual input. It should be admitted that throughout the history of philosophy, the arts and literature, certain male authors and artists have cast women in the role of 'Muse' who inspires their intellectual or artistic creation, a framing of women's roles that often involves much objectification. There are at least two major problems with minimising the role of ancient women philosophers as catalysts in this way: firstly, in relation to the Platonic tradition, it must be noted that inspiration was valued far more highly and was seen as much more closely connected to intellectual endeavour than in other (ancient and modern) philosophical traditions.[127] This valuation applies not only in relation to religious practice and theurgy, but also with regard to the inspiration which was often framed as a significant catalyst for philosophical investigation, such as the Delphic Oracle which catalysed Socrates' philosophical practice and use of elenchus (see Section 1.1.2). Thus, when Platonist women philosophers are presented as inspiring the production of a philosophical work it is important not to minimise

---

[126] See Langlands 2004: 118, who compares Seneca's *Ad Marcellam* with a similar work in the same genre, a consolation to a male addressee, Polybius.

[127] I thank Danielle Layne, Michael Griffin and Sonsoles Costero-Quiroga for discussion of this point (personal correspondence, 29 November 2024).

this role in relation to contemporary notions of 'inspiration'. This is especially the case when women philosophers were priestesses, or priestess-like figures, such as Clea was (see Section 5.2).

In addition, it is vital to take epistemic injustice into account when analysing women's roles as catalysts of male-authored works. As discussed, women's roles in philosophical textual production have often been elided or minimised. As explored in relation to Timoxena and Hypatia, women's philosophical writings have sometimes been attributed to male philosophers who were their relatives or associates. To these examples, we might add the ancient female mathematician Pandrosion, well-respected enough to attract pupils and to be the addressee of a work by Pappus, but as Grainne McLoughlin (2004: 17–20) argues, 'she has been edited out of existence as part and parcel of the editorial-decision making process' because several modern editors and translators of Pappus' work assumed she must be male. Consequently, it is vital to factor into any assessment of women's roles – including their roles as significant catalysts of male-authored texts – the historical minimisation or elision of women's intellectual contributions within the western philosophical tradition, science and the academy.[128] To be clear, within a wider context, women's contributions to intellectual investigation and philosophical writings (whether authored by them or their male colleagues) have, historically, been minimised largely because of epistemic injustice. We might add that the experience of systematic, persistent testimonial injustice may have led ancient women to pass on their own philosophical ideas to male colleagues to publish, as discussed in relation to Clea. Given the historical minimisation of women's intellectual contributions within the western philosophical tradition, science and the academy, we should apply extra caution to any interpretation that has the effect of minimising women's intellectual contributions. Indeed, it would be advisable to factor in awareness of historical epistemic injustice as a methodological principle when assessing women's roles in textual production.

Utilising conceptions of instrumental, collective and relational agency can act as a corrective to instances of epistemic injustice which have elided or downplayed the contributions of women. Furthermore, these concepts of agency may entail that we need to re-think the way in which we attribute philosophical ideas to specific individuals rather than communities. As Caterina Pellò and Katharine O'Reilly (2023: 17) note,

> The general strategy in the history of philosophy has been to focus on great minds to whom we can more confidently ascribe particular philosophical ideas ... and discuss philosophical communities as a kind of outgrowth of the

---
[128] See McHardy & Marshall 2004: 2–3; McLaughlin 2004: 7–25.

thought and influence of these prominent figures ... These trends suppress the role of philosophical communities and especially those members whose individual contributions are not independently recorded.

They argue that an alternative approach is to think more holistically about the development of philosophical theories and the role that we can attribute to those of any gender identity, partially by focusing on school doctrines rather than individual authorship, cautioning that 'If woman were active members of philosophical communities, we should resist the assumption that their presence was merely as passive followers' by considering evidence to the contrary, since, even when we lack specifics, we have evidence that women contributed to forming and developing the ideas ascribed to these schools (O'Reilly & Pellò 2023: 16–17).

4.3 Conclusion

Using the philosophical writings of Hypatia and Timoxena as case studies, I suggest that some works authored by Platonist women philosophers may have been transmitted anonymously or attributed to a related male philosopher. These methodological questions relating to women's writings merit further examination in relation to the specific – but also diverse and variable – historical and cultural contexts relating to processes of textual preservation and transmission. Women in later Platonism also made significant contributions to the Platonic tradition in terms of catalysing the production of male-authored texts. In doing so, they exercised a considerable instrumental agency in ensuring that specific philosophical figures, questions or topics received detailed treatment.

5 Platonic Philosopher-Priestesses

From Diotima onwards, many women associated with Platonism are presented as *both* philosophers and priestesses. The Platonic tradition seems to have been influenced by the close relationship between philosophy and religion in Pythagorean communities in this regard. For instance, Aristoxenus reports that Pythagoras was taught by the Delphic priestess Themistoklea (D.L. 8.8, 8.21). From the Roman imperial period onwards, historical women associated with Platonism are often presented as philosopher-priestesses, following the example of the paradigmatic philosopher-priestess: Plato's Diotima. Scholars of philosophy have tended to overlook entirely the range of philosopher-priestesses associated with the Platonic tradition. When scholars pay any attention to this trend, it is often dismissed as a fictitious literary trope and/or as philosophically insignificant. This section will challenge both claims.

Epigraphic evidence from the Roman imperial period shows that some historical women were presented as both philosophers and priestesses, thus undermining the claim that this trend is merely a literary trope (Addey 2022: 20–22, 2024: 465–466). Drawing on recent work that has reassessed the complementarity of ancient religious and ritual practices within Platonist philosophy, this section aims to reassess the importance of these women within the development and major trajectories of Platonism.

5.1 Diotima of Mantinea: The Prototype Philosopher-Priestess

When Socrates reports Diotima's teaching in Plato's *Symposium*, the latter's ritual expertise is emphasised from the outset. He introduces Diotima as a 'wise woman' (σοφὴ) who is skilled concerning Eros and 'many other matters' (ἄλλα πολλά) (*Symp.* 201d2-3). This description recalls Socrates' claim in Plato's *Meno* that he learnt many things 'from priests and priestesses who have studied so as to be able to give a reasoned account of their ministry' (81a10-b1). He refers to these priests and priestesses specifically as 'wise men and women' (*Meno* 81a5-6: ἀνδρῶν τε καὶ γυναικῶν σοφῶν), who discuss 'divine matters' (θεῖα πράγματα). The association with the priesthood is solidified by Socrates' emphasis on Diotima's ritual service for the Athenians, where she advised them to make certain sacrifices to offset or delay the plague (*Symp.* 201d7-8). This ritual expertise indicates that Diotima was a seer: both independent seers and those connected with oracular sanctuaries offered divinatory advice to Greek people and communities which often focused on treating individual or collective forms of disease.

Diotima is implicitly presented as a seer throughout Socrates' speech in Plato's *Symposium* (201d, 206b11-12), particularly by the pun on the name of her place of origin, since Μαντινικῆς (the 'Mantinean') is similar to the Greek term for 'divination' (μάντικη) (*Symp.* 201d5).[129] Diotima comments on the workings of divination when she claims that *daimones* bring divinatory messages from the gods to humans (202e13). As a priestess, Diotima's discourse is infused appropriately with religious language and themes. Her speech is structured in relation to the stages of initiation in the mystery cult at Eleusis (Burkert 1987: 70). Nancy Evans (2006: 2) has explored the ways in which Diotima is like the goddess Demeter, as a sort of mystagogue who initiates individuals into her mysteries and mediates information about the divine to humans. Diotima's speech is inclusive in terms of the religious practices it references: these include those relating to the Eleusinian mystery cult, but also civic, public religious practices (202e8-203a9).

---

[129] Evans 2006: 8; Addey 2024: 463–464.

Recent scholars have largely doubted Diotima's status as a historical figure; the current consensus is that she is fictitious (see Section 2.1.1). One argument offered to support this apparent fictionality is that 'Plato could never have met this foreign woman who is said to have known Socrates before Plato was born and is otherwise absent from the historical record' (Nails 2015: 74). Debra Nails notes the weakness of this defence of fictionality, firstly because it is an argument from silence and, secondly, because Plato often wrote accounts of historical figures he could only have known by reputation (Nails 2015: 74). As noted, non-Athenians would be less likely to appear in the extant historical record, given that most of our evidence for classical Greece comes from Athens (Levin 1975: 225).

In denying Diotima's historicity, scholars may have been influenced by the lack of importance of priestesses in mainstream, 'Western' contemporary cultures and religions, as well as by the elision or denial of the significance of the connections between philosophy and religion within the Platonic tradition. After all, the two most common assumptions made about Diotima – that she is either Aspasia in disguise or fictitious – both minimise the historical significance of priestesses in classical Greek culture and religion, and downplay the significant connections between religion and philosophy in Plato. Diotima was assumed to have been an actual person until the early modern period (Nails 2015: 73–75). Yet, since that time, no other character in Plato has been treated with such scepticism. However, recent scholarship has re-assessed the important public roles which priestesses played in archaic, classical and Hellenistic religion and culture, and in the Roman imperial period across the Mediterranean basin. Joan Breton Connelly demonstrates (by combining relevant epigraphic, literary and archaeological evidence) that priestesses were authoritative public office-holders with a much broader level of civic engagement than has previously been recognised (Connelly 2007: 276–278). In terms of Diotima's possible historicity, the social conventions of fifth-century Athens which usually prohibited unsupervised contact between (non-related) aristocratic men and women would not apply to Socrates' conversation with Diotima if the latter was indeed a priestess.

If Diotima was a historical woman, she may have been a priestess of Apollo: some scholars have linked a marble votive relief and statue of a priestess found at Mantinea with Diotima.[130] This statue (dated to 425–400 BCE) is displayed in the National Museum of Athens as the 'Stele of Diotima', even though the identification is speculative (see Figure 1).[131] It depicts a woman engaging in

---

[130] Möbius 1934: 45–60; Robinson & Blegen 1935: 389.
[131] On the dating of the statue, see Nails 2015: 75.

Platonist Women 63

Figure 1 The Stele of Diotima. National Archaeological Museum 226, Athens. © Hellenic Ministry of Culture / Hellenic Organization of Cultural Resources Development.

a very specific ritual action: she holds a liver in her hands, suggesting she is engaged in haruspicy, divination involving reading animal entrails – the presence of a palm tree in the background strengthens the association with Apollo, the god of divination (Connelly 2007: 238–240).

The relief was found in the agora at Mantinea which suggests it may have been votive, although its size and the high relief of the sculpture are comparable to funerary monuments. Cuttings on the edge of the slab suggest it may have been re-positioned at some point, possibly moved from the cemetery to the agora to honour a special priestess or prophetess publicly – Diotima (Connelly 2007: 240). Given the content of her speech in Plato's *Symposium*, it is also possible that Diotima might have been a priestess of the Eleusinian mystery cult (Nails 2015: 74), of Artemis (Layne 2024) or of the Eleusinian Demeter in Arcadia (Addey 2024: 464).

As discussed in Section 2, Diotima teaches Socrates about the nature of Eros as a 'great *daimon*' who, like other *daimones*, is an intermediary being who mediates between gods and mortals (*Symp.* 203e2-3). Nancy Evans has emphasised that the priestess' or seer's relation with other people constitutes another type of divine mediation, as when the Athenians learned the god's will about the plague through Diotima, who utilised divination to interpret the god's will to them (Evans 2006: 12). Diotima embodies the daimonic through her ritual action and teaching. She defines the philosopher as the one who seeks wisdom and identifies Eros himself as a philosopher or 'friend of wisdom' (204b4). Overall, the content of Diotima's discourse presents the task of the philosopher as mediating between the divine and human: Diotima herself takes on this role in her teaching of Socrates, which has an initiatory quality. The religious and philosophical transmission from teacher to pupil, exemplified here by Diotima and taken up by philosopher-priestesses within later Platonism, is presented as 'daimonic', that is to say, as mimicking the mediating action of Eros. Joan Breton Connelly has examined the recurring depiction of male philosophers receiving advice from prophetesses in ancient Greece and concludes that priestly women, well-respected for their learning and wise counsel, may have played significant historical roles as teachers and advisors of men (Connelly 2007: 220).

Within Diotima's discourse, we see female to male inter-generational transmission in Diotima's teaching of Socrates. In her roles as ritual expert and philosophical teacher, the portrayal of Diotima influenced the roles of many historical women associated with later Platonism, who also take on the role of 'philosopher-priestess'. Therefore, whether Diotima is fictitious or historical, she is an important figure in the history of philosophy and her role as a prototype philosopher-priestess influenced historical women associated with later Platonism *and* the development of the religious direction of later Platonism.

5.2 Clea of Delphi: The Philosopher-Priestess in Middle Platonism

As discussed, Clea was the dedicatee and addressee of Plutarch's *On Isis and Osiris* and *Virtues in Women*. In the former, we hear that Clea was a priestess, the leader of the Dionysian *thyias* at Delphi and an initiate of the Isis cult (*On Isis and Osiris* 364e2-6, 351e9-f2, 352c2-8). Clea and Plutarch had clearly become friends as a result of their shared commitment to priestly duties at Delphi. At a mature age, Plutarch served as a priest of Apollo at Delphi for several decades, which entailed active involvement in ritual acts including 'sacrificing, leading processions and taking part in a chorus' (*An seni* 792 f).

Clea is extremely significant because she is the first philosopher-priestess within the Platonic tradition attested with certainty in the historical record. Two inscriptions from Delphi name Flavia Clea: the first records a dedication of a statue by Flavia Clea to her mother Eurydice and is dated to the first quarter of the second century CE.¹³² The second inscription records another dedication by Flavia Clea – who has the title ἡ ἀρχηίς – of a statue to Matidia II, the emperor's aunt, and dates to the reign of Antoninus Pius (138–161 CE).¹³³ The fact that Flavia Clea is given the title ἀρχηίς indicates that she was a priestess at Delphi, and a leader of the Thyiades. Some scholars identify Flavia Clea with the dedicatee of Plutarch's works.¹³⁴ However, there may be a problem with the chronology since Flavia Clea would have been young when Leontis died and Plutarch treats his dedicatee as a close friend (and Leontis as their mutual friend), addressing her with great respect (Kapetanopoulos 1966: 129 n.5). On this basis, some have proposed that Plutarch's addressee Clea is actually the mother – or mother-in-law – of Eurydice and the grandmother of Flavia Clea.¹³⁵ This Clea may be the same woman mentioned in another inscription from Daulis in Phocis, near Delphi (*IG* IX, 1, 61, l. 20-22).¹³⁶ Yet it is possible that Plutarch would indeed have treated a much younger women (i.e. Flavia Clea) with such respect, given that she was invested with the religious and cultural authority of a priestess. However, if the dedicatee of Plutarch's works is to be identified with Eurydice's mother (or mother-in-law) – and the grandmother of Flavia Clea – then she was also ἀρχηίς, the leader of the Thyiades at Delphi, and we see the transmission of religious roles and expertise, as well as philosophical knowledge, amongst these three generations of Middle Platonic women (Clea – Eurydice – Flavia Clea). If Plutarch's dedicatee is rather Flavia Clea, it seems significant that in the epigraphic record there is evidence of her honouring other women (her mother Eurydice and the emperor's aunt), given that Plutarch's addressee catalysed and encouraged Plutarch to write his work *Virtues in Women*, to honour their friend Leontis and other virtuous women. Thus, traces of female-to-female religio-philosophical transmission in Middle Platonism emerge from epigraphic evidence, as well as from Plutarch's texts.

In *On Isis and Osiris*, Clea's role as a philosopher-priestess emerges most emphatically, alongside the influence of Diotima upon Clea, who will join Plutarch in his search for knowledge of the gods, framed as the greatest blessing the gods can give (*On Isis and Osiris* 351 c-d). This work cites Diotima's speech and her view of *daimones* as intermediaries between gods and mortals (361c1-5) as part of a wider consideration of the nature of *daimones* (360d–361d), and the myth of Eros' birth from Poverty and Plenty (374c9-d10), in a manner which suggests that Clea, as Plutarch's interlocutor, is fully conversant with Diotima's

---

[132] *SEG* 1, 159. See Bowersock 1965: 267.
[133] For the text of this inscription, see Jannoray 1946: 254–259.
[134] Bowersock 1965: 267–268; Jones 1966; Russell 1973: 6.
[135] Kapetaneopoulos 1966: 129–130 n.5; Puech 1992: 4842; Stadter 1999.
[136] See Kapetanopoulos 1966: 129–130 n.5.

discourse in Plato's *Symposium*. Plutarch, in conversation with Clea, presents the gaining of philosophical insight as an epoptic experience, drawing on Diotima's characterisation of the philosophic ascent:

> But the apperception of the conceptual, the pure and the simple, shining through the soul like a flash of lightning, affords an opportunity to touch and see it but once. For this reason Plato and Aristotle call this part of philosophy the epoptic or mystic part, inasmuch as those who have passed beyond these conjectural and confused matters of all sorts by means of Reason proceed by leaps and bound to that primary, simple and immaterial principle ... (*On Isis and Osiris* 382d5-12. Trans. Babbit 1936)[137]

The presentation of philosophy as a mystogogic path draws explicitly on Diotima's teaching in the *Symposium*. In a wider sense, the way in which Plutarch in conversation with Clea within this work juxtaposes explanations of religious cult and customs alongside philosophical investigation draws extensively on the mode of religio-philosophical transmission exemplified by Plato's Diotima. Additionally, Diotima, in her role as a philosopher-priestess, may well have inspired Clea in her own philosophical and religious roles and activities.

5.3 Female Theurgists as Philosopher-Priestesses in Neoplatonism

It is clear that female theurgists – presented as philosopher-priestesses – played significant roles in the development of theurgy in later Neoplatonism. Their involvement has to be considered as part of a broader pattern that emerges in late antiquity: the rise of the 'holy man' (θεῖος ἀνήρ) and 'holy woman' (or to use a gender-neutral term, 'person of power'), who acted as a link between human communities and the divine, and whose presence is evident across multiple late antique religious traditions, including traditional Mediterranean 'pagan' religions and early Christianity.[138]

Diotima's persona – and the content of her teaching in Plato's *Symposium* – implicitly affected the development of theurgy (Addey 2024: 467–470). The *Symposium* was central to Iamblichus' canon of Plato's works: the dialogue held the penultimate place in the first cycle of dialogues (Anon. *Proleg.* 26.12-34), and thus was important within the late Neoplatonist teaching curriculum. As such, it would have been taught by Iamblichus, by Plutarch of Athens, Syrianus and Proclus within the Athenian School, and by Olympiodorus and others in the

---

[137] See also *On Isis and Osiris* 378a11-b8.
[138] On the rise of the late antique 'holy man': see Brown 1971: 80–101; Fowden 1982: 33–59; Cox 1983; Athanassiadi 2013: 13–27. On the gender issues involved, see Bingham-Kolenkow 2002: 133–144; Tanaseanu-Döbler 2013: 123–147.

Alexandrian School (Anon. *Proleg.* 26.17-18). Therefore, Sosipatra and Asclepigeneia would certainly have been familiar with this work and the portrayal of Diotima therein.

5.3.1 Female Theurgists in the Neoplatonic Schools in Pergamon and Athens

Two female theurgists stand out as philosopher-priestesses: Sosipatra, who became Head of the Neoplatonic School at Pergamon alongside Aedesius, and Asclepigeneia, a teacher of theurgy in the Athenian School.

Sosipatra is presented as a seer and theurgist, as well as a philosopher, by Eunapius, who characterises her as a priestess-like figure (Addey 2018: 144–161). In the way that she combines these roles, Sosipatra was influenced by Diotima's status as a philosopher-priestess.[139] Sosipatra is consistently characterised as a 'divine' or 'holy woman': Eunapius may well present Sosipatra as a counter-portrait of the 'holy woman' in contrast to the Christian ideal of the celibate female ascetic who does not marry or have children (Marx 2021: 14–15).

Sosipatra's status as a seer is a major feature of Eunapius' account: she had an ability which can be characterised as psychic, clairvoyant power, an unusual phenomenon in Graeco-Roman antiquity (Addey 2018: 144–145). In the episode which occurs when Sosipatra is teaching about the immortality and descent of the soul (see Section 3.2.1), she is depicted as entering an inspired state described as 'Korybantic and bacchic frenzy', where she related her vision of her student Philometer's carriage accident (*VS* 6.9.12.5-14.1). Here, we see that Sosipatra moved easily between a discursive mode of discourse and inspired, divinatory utterance (Addey 2018: 152–153). Sosipatra's expertise suggests that divination and epistemology were closely connected in her teaching and practice (Addey 2018). Eunapius relates several similar episodes which display Sosipatra's divinatory insight into past, present and future (*VS* 6.7.3.2-6.7.5.3; 6.8.3.3-6.8.5.3).[140] Her ritual expertise clearly influenced her son Antoninus, who also became a 'holy man' – he went to Egypt, devoted himself to ritual practices in Canobus, and prophesied the destruction of the Temple of Serapis in Alexandria (*VS* 6.9.15.2-17.8; 6.10.6-6.11.3).

Because Sosipatra does not actively perform rituals in Eunapius' biography, Sarah Iles Johnston has argued that she is 'passive' because her inspiration is spontaneous rather than ritually induced (Johnston 2012: 110). Yet, Sosipatra was trained in ritual and initiated by the Chaldeans as a child: after they leave,

---

[139] For a detailed examination of Diotima's influence on Sosipatra, see Addey 2024.
[140] Addey 2018: 153-154, 2024: 472–475.

she is said to be 'fully initiated' (τεθειασμένην) and 'divinely inspired' (σωφρόνως ἐνθουσιῶσαν) – and so ritual practices form a consistent cornerstone of her expertise.[141] Sosipatra is implicitly characterised as an advanced theurgist whose expertise encompasses physical forms of ritual as well as intellectual worship, since these stages of theurgic ritual were considered cumulative and integrative.[142] Her oracular visions are presented as spontaneous because her whole life has become ritualistic: she is depicted as constantly connected to the gods through her receptivity and inspiration, and thus able to hear their oracular advice consistently (Addey 2018: 151). When Sosipatra asks Maximus of Ephesus to perform a ritual on her behalf to dispel Philometer's love magic, we see her teaching Maximus about the appropriate context, ethics and timing of theurgic ritual.[143]

When considering Sosipatra's religious context and role as a philosopher-priestess, it should be noted that since at least the Hellenistic period, priestesses had played a significant role in the religious and civic life of Pergamon, where they were commemorated with statues and dedicatory inscriptions during the Hellenistic and Roman periods. Two inscriptions from Pergamon are dedicated to a woman called Sosipatra, who was a priestess. The first inscription (found on the slope below the Great Altar near the theatre) is on a statue base of a bronze statue: it is a dedication from the people of Pergamon to Sosipatra, the daughter of Menophiles, who is designated as a priestess of Athena Polias and Nicephoros – interestingly, she is praised for her moderation (σωφροσύνη), virtue (ἀρετή) and holiness (εὐσέβεια), qualities often attributed to philosophers (male and female) in the epigraphic record.[144] The second inscription is dedicated to a woman called Sosipatra described as a priestess and may refer to the same woman as the first (*I. Pergamon* VIII, 2, no. 488.). Both inscriptions have been dated to the first or second century BCE, which means that this is not our Sosipatra. However, it is extremely likely to have been her ancestor since the Neoplatonic Sosipatra had a family estate in Pergamon and these are the only two women with the name attested in coastal Asia Minor in antiquity (Corsten 2010: 419). Therefore, Sosipatra was likely descended from a well-known Hellenistic priestess of Athena of the same name.

It is also possible that the bronze triangular table or base discovered as part of a divination kit excavated from Pergamon (dated to the late third century CE) may have been a theurgic ritual tool linked with Sosipatra, Aedesius and the

---

[141] Eunapius, *VS* 6.7.1-2; 6.7.8.2-6.7.9.1; 6.8.1.2-3; Addey 2018: 150.

[142] Iamblichus, *DM* 5.26 (240.9-13). See Addey 2018: 150–151.

[143] *VS* 6.9.3.1-6.9.8.1. See Addey 2018: 151–152.

[144] *I.Pergamon* VIII.2, no. 492, ed. Frankel 1895. See Eule 2001: 92–95; Connelly 2007: 140.

Neoplatonic School at Pergamon.[145] As well as the triangular base, the kit contains an engraved bronze disc, two lamellae, two rings, a large bronze nail and three black stones containing inscriptions and *charakteres*.[146] Wünsch argued that the kit was owned by a magician who used each item within a single ritual: the disc was placed on a post on the triangular base and was used as an alphabet oracle with the suspended ring (Wünsch 1905: 39–40). However, there are major problems with this theory, especially the fact that the signs on the disc do not follow a comprehensible alphabetical or ideographical system (Gordon 2002: 189–190).

The triangular base contains a depiction of a goddess holding two cultic objects in her hands in each of its three corners, each labelled above with an epithet: Dione (who holds a whip and torch), Phoibie (a key and torch) and Nykhie (a serpent and dagger); at the foot of each figure is the word *Am(e)ibousa* (= *Ameibousa*) 'the changing one' (fem.), while the remaining surface of the table is covered with words, groups of vowels and *charakteres*, including the magical names of Artemis, Persephone and Hekate, and *Leukophryene*, the cultic epithet of Artemis of Magnesia (see Figure 2).

Figure 2 The Divination Kit from Pergamon: triangular base and disc.
© ANTIKENSAMMLUNG, STAATLICHE MUSEEN ZU BERLIN –
PREUSSISCHER KULTURBESITZ. Misc.8612, 5.
Photographer: Ingrid Geske.

---

[145] For the dating of the Pergamon kit, see Wünsch 1905: 20. The connection with theurgy is suggested by Mastrocinque 2002: 173–187; Jackson 2012: 457–474.
[146] Wünsch 1905; Mastrocinque 2002: 174–176.

Based on these labels, the figures' dress and the objects they carry, the figures have been identified as the three aspects of triple Hekate (Jackson 2012: 455). The divinatory function of the triangular base is suggested by the epithets Dione, Phoibie and Nykhie, which relate to Hekate's oracular powers: Dione was Zeus' consort goddess at the oracle of Dodona, Phoibie was linked with Phoibus Apollo and Delphi, while Nykhie was an oracular deity.[147] Although we do not know precisely how the triangular base was utilised, it may have been used for theurgic statue animation and divination, with a statuette of the deity placed on the base and then animated ritually to provide divinatory messages to the theurgist.[148]

That this ritual tool might be linked with Sosipatra, Aedesius and their School is suggested by the central role of Hekate in the Chaldean Oracles, a foundational text for Neoplatonic theurgy. In the Chaldean Oracles, Hekate is an oracular goddess who delivers some of the oracles but also features in the extant fragments as an intermediary goddess of life between the First and Second Fathers.[149] Furthermore, a very similar bronze triangular base was excavated at the Maison du Cerf in Apamea in 1977, which had been destroyed by fire in the sixth century CE, although the letter-forms on the base suggest it was inscribed in the second or third century CE (Donnay 1984: 203). This triangular base is slightly smaller than the Pergamene specimen and was badly damaged in the fire but one corner survives unscathed and shows a three-headed goddess figure carrying a whip and torch labelled 'Dione' above and '*Amibousa*' below, similar to the Pergamene table (Donnay 1984: 203–204). The geographic provenance of these triangular tables suggests that they were used by theurgists associated with Iamblichus' School in Apamea. Attilio Mastrocinque has argued that the Pergamene triangular base and disc represent a miniature universe modelled on Plato's Myth of Er and links these tools with Maximus of Ephesus (Mastrocinque 2002: 180–183). However, Sosipatra's connections with the Chaldean tradition and with Pergamon suggest that she may well have used the Pergamon triangular base for theurgic divination, and passed on this ritual tool to Maximus.

---

[147] Donnay 1984: 205–207; Jackson 2012: 462–464.

[148] For an important ritual parallel see *PGM* IV. 1909-11, 1840-1870, 1877-1901 (statuettes of Eros); Gordon 2002: 193–194.

[149] Jackson 2012: 470–471, notes that some attributes on the triangular base represent Hekate's underworldly aspects rather than her celestial qualities more typically associated with the Chaldean Oracles. Yet late antique theurgists did not demarcate strictly the celestial and chthonic aspects of deities like Hekate. Even within the Chaldean Oracles, Hekate is depicted as ruler of the *daimones*, and associated with *physis,* nature and Fate.

Sosipatra seems to have influenced Asclepigeneia, who is presented as a crucial link in the lineage and chain of transmission of theurgy within the Athenian School:

> For he [i.e. Proclus] made use of the conjunctions and supplications of the Chaldaeans, together with their divine and ineffable revolutions. These he acquired for himself, and from Asclepigeneia, the daughter of Plutarch, he learned the invocations and the rest of the apparatus. For she alone preserved the rituals, and the whole process of theurgy, handed on to her from the great Nestorius by her father. (Marinus, *Proc.* 28.9-15, trans. Edwards 2000)

She taught Proclus theurgy, passing on the ritual expertise and knowledge of Chaldean tradition which she learned from her father, Plutarch of Athens, and which he in turn had learned from her grandfather Nestorius, who had been a seer and a hierophant of the mystery cult at Eleusis.[150] Asclepigeneia, a descendant of the priest Nestorius, is characterised as an expert theurgist, a philosopher-priestess figure. Additionally, Asclepigeneia may have been a priestess of Asclepius: her father had a family cult to this god and their house was next to 'the shrine of Asclepius celebrated by Sophocles' (*Proc.* 29).[151]

Asclepigeneia's transmission of ritual procedures to Proclus entails intergenerational female to male transmission of ritual and philosophical expertise modelled on Diotima's bestowal of initiatory knowledge to Socrates in the *Symposium*. Given that Plato's Diotima presented the philosopher's ascent to the Form of Beauty using the language and terminology of the Eleusinian mysteries, reflecting the idea that Diotima's 'ladder of love' represents an initiatory ascent, it is interesting that Asclepigeneia is linked implicitly with the Eleusinian mysteries through Nestorius. Asclepigeneia is also characterised as an expert in Chaldean ritual practices and tools. In this respect, Diotima's emphasis on Eros (and *erōs* as desire and longing for the beautiful and Beauty itself) is mirrored in and may have influenced the Chaldean Oracles. Within the Chaldean Oracles, *erōs* has an important role as a cosmic principle and as a central psychological element of the human soul which catalyses its return to the intelligible realm (fr. 42-44). Thus, Diotima's 'ladder of love' seems to have influenced the formation of the central goal of theurgy, the ascent of the soul to the divine, intelligible realm, while Diotima – in her role as a philosopher-priestess – acted as a role model for Asclepigeneia and Sosipatra. As discussed, Eunapius emphasises Sosipatra's unconventional education by Chaldean strangers, linking

---

[150] On Nestorius, see Marinus, *Proc.* 12; Eunapius, *VS* 475-76, 493; Zosimus 4.18; Clinton 1974: 43; Burkert 1987: 50, 85, 113–114; Addey 2014a: 280; Watts 2017: 53–54.

[151] Edwards 2000: 100 n. 295; Slaveva-Griffin 2016: 185.

her with the Chaldean tradition and, by implication, the Chaldean Oracles (*VS* 6.6.7.1-6.7.11.5).

Asclepigeneia may be the unnamed 'Athenian women' mentioned by Damascius (*Phil. Hist.* fr. 104B). The identification is suggested by related fragments of the text which refer to ritual activity, such as a 'supernatural earthquake' which may describe Proclus' use of theurgic ritual to defend against earthquakes or the related theurgic skills of his teacher, Asclepigeneia.[152] A further fragment states, 'She prays to the god to give her truly holy counsel, and advice on what to do' which relates to a request for divinatory advice (fr. 104 C). The Athenian woman is said to be 'much skilled in the art of persuasion (εἰς πειθώ)' (fr. 104B). It is tempting to relate this to Emperor Julian's injunction to the priestess Theodora that the duty of a spiritual leader is 'to persuade and save' (*Ep.* 86, 33-34: πείθειν καὶ σώζειν). Although Asclepigeneia is not named specifically, if these fragments refer to her, they strengthen the attribution of considerable ritual expertise to her.

5.3.2 Philosopher-Priestesses and Julian's Religious Restoration

Women – particularly philosopher-priestesses – played an important role within Emperor Julian's religious restoration (361–363 CE), which attempted to revitalise traditional 'pagan' Mediterranean religion in the face of its marginalisation and the competition stemming from the Christianisation of the Roman Empire in the fourth century CE. It is well-recognised that Julian's dedication to theurgy and Neoplatonism influenced his religious restoration. Julian himself had been educated by Iamblichus' philosophic successors who were also theurgists: particularly Chrysanthius of Sardis and Maximus of Ephesus. We do not know if Julian met or was taught by Sosipatra; Eunapius never mentions her when reporting Julian's visit to Aedesius in Pergamon. Nevertheless, Sosipatra is presented as a teacher of Maximus of Ephesus, who taught Julian, so she may have had an indirect influence on the parameters of Julian's religious project.

Julian's efforts to restore traditional temples across the Roman Empire very much included priestesses. His correspondents included Theodora, a priestess who played an important role in the religious restoration. Theodora was well-educated and engaged in philosophy: she sent Julian philosophical books and letters (*Ep.* 32, 1-2; 33, 1-2) and Julian calls her 'wisdom itself' (*Ep.* 34, 1). As a priestess, Theodora took her sacred duties very seriously: Julian calls her 'most reverent' (*Ep.* 33) and describes her 'generosity of soul' in entreating the gods on his behalf and informing him of the blessings revealed (*Ep.* 34, 4-7).

---

[152] Damascius, *Phil. Hist.* fr. 104A; Athanassiadi 1999: 251 nn.275-76.

Theodora's ritual service included prayers on behalf of Julian and his religious restoration; Julian's allusion to 'blessings' refers to Theodora's use of divination and the propitious omens or divinatory messages she received. Julian also wrote to Kallixene, a priestess of Demeter at Pessinus in Phrygia, whom he honoured with a second priesthood, that of Cybele (*Ep.* 42, 389a).

5.3.3 Female Theurgists in Alexandria

The question of Hypatia's possible engagement in theurgy is contested. Until recently, the consensus was that she worked in the tradition of Plotinus and had little to do with theurgy or the religious aspects of Neoplatonism.[153] There seems to be some minimisation of her status as pagan in scholarship, probably in response to the distorting nature of later European literature which used her as an instrument of religious polemic.[154] Yet Hypatia remained pagan throughout her life, even though converting to Christianity would have made her teaching and intellectual activities far easier within the context of Alexandria.[155] Of course, an ancient philosopher could be pagan without necessarily being a theurgist, but the elision of her religious background may suggest some minimisation of the religious aspects of her teaching. Alan Cameron and Jacqueline Long have argued that Hypatia and Theon were adepts of Iamblichean Neoplatonism, steeped in the Chaldean Oracles which were inextricably linked with theurgy; Hypatia may have learned theurgy from Antoninus, Sosipatra's son, after he moved to Egypt (Cameron & Long 1993: 44, 58–60). The *Suda* entry attesting Hypatia's writings implies her expertise in astronomy and astrology, in addition to mathematics and philosophy. The interest in theurgic ritual and divination, specifically the Chaldean Oracles and dream divination, displayed by Hypatia's pupil Synesius is also suggestive.[156] Synesius reports that Hypatia taught him how to make an astrolabe, an instrument associated with astrology (*De dono* 311a) and refers to Hypatia's 'oracular utterance' (*Ep.* 5, 305-308) which might indicate that he considers her teaching as inspired. However, Damascius does not describe Hypatia as a theurgist or report her engaging with any ritual practices, although his text is fragmentary (Schultz 2023: 204). Overall, the issue is uncertain but there are some indications that Hypatia may have been interested in theurgy.

Damascius depicts several women associated with Neoplatonism in Alexandria as theurgists or philosopher-priestess figures, such as the seer

---

[153] Dzielska 1995: 63; Watts 2017: 43; Geertz 2020: 142.
[154] See Dzielska 1995: 46, who calls Hypatia 'indifferent to pagan cults'.
[155] Alexandria was a majority Christian city by the time Hypatia was teaching: see Watts 2017: 47.
[156] Synesius, *De insomniis* 135b, 140b. See Addey 2022: 28.

Anthusa who discovered the method of divination by clouds (*Phil, Hist.* fr. 52). We also hear about Aedesia, a relative of Syrianus and Hermeias' wife (fr. 57B-C), whom Damascius met in the 480s CE when he was a student in Horapollo's school. At this point, Aedesia was a widow associated with this school and one of the personalities who gave the school 'a distinctive aura as a citadel of . . . paganism' (Athanassiadi 1999: 22). Damascius characterises Aedesia as 'truly exceptional . . . in her love and care for the divine and for humanity', qualities exemplified in her commitment to charity (fr. 56, 5). He emphasises her justice and moderation, two of the Platonic virtues (fr. 56, 3-5). Aedesia's dedication to helping those in poverty is unparalleled in extant accounts of Neoplatonist philosophers. She showed considerable independence in continuing this charity after Hermeias' death and in the face of criticism for leaving her sons in debt (fr. 56, 5-14). However, Damascius highlights Aedesia's care for her sons' education, including the unique achievement of managing to retain the maintenance from her husband's public paid chair for them (fr. 56, 15-21; see Section 3.2.2).

Aedesia is exemplary in her attempt to develop the political-civic grade of virtue, through her charity work 'to realise her ideal of justice' (Schultz 2022: 128). In this respect, she is presented as an empowered ethical role model in a similar manner to Timoxena. Significantly, Damascius hints that Aedesia was a theurgist by seemingly depicting her attainment of hieratic or theurgic virtue.[157] Specifically, he emphasises Aedesia's exceptional 'love of god' (φιλόθεον) and 'care for humanity' (φιλάνθρωπον), qualities associated in later Neoplatonism with the attainment of hieratic or theurgic virtue since they were considered to be the embodied expression of the theurgist's assimilation to the divine (fr. 56, 5). This impression is reinforced by Damascius' characterisation of Aedesia as pious, holy, and so 'beloved of the gods' that she received many divine epiphanies (fr. 56, 26-27).

5.4 Conclusion

Diotima stands as the prototype philosopher-priestess within the Platonic tradition. Her teaching envisages philosophy as an initiatory path based on the power of *erōs* to unite humans, ultimately, with the intelligible and divine world of the Forms. While her status as a historical or fictitious figure is contested, Diotima – both in her role as philosopher-priestess and in relation to the content of her teaching in Plato's *Symposium* – had an important influence on later historical philosopher-priestesses within Middle Platonism and Neoplatonism

---

[157] Damascius' reticence about identifying theurgists explicitly may relate to theurgy going 'underground' in the wake of the Theodosian decrees and the increasing persecution of 'pagans' in his time: see Denzey-Lewis 2014: 289, 292. On the persecution of 'pagans' and fraught atmosphere in Alexandria in the 480s CE, see Athanassiadi 1999: 24–29.

from the Roman imperial period onwards. Clea is especially significant as the first philosopher-priestess associated with Platonism whose historical status is attested with certainty. The way in which Clea is presented in *On Isis and Osiris* suggests that she, like Plutarch, conceived of philosophy as an initiatory experience in a manner influenced by Diotima's discourse. In late antiquity, we see the religious-philosophical focus of Platonism elaborated in the emergence of theurgy and the corresponding importance of female theurgists, depicted as philosopher-priestess figures, who acted as crucial links in theurgic lineage and transmission. Yet Clea serves to remind us that the connections between religion and philosophy, and the philosopher-priestess, pre-date the development of theurgy. The figure of the philosopher-priestess is important throughout the Platonic tradition.

6 Conclusion: The Significance of Platonist Women

This Element has explored the roles of Platonist women within the Platonic tradition, re-assessing their epistemic agency and significance. These women variously played important and multifaceted roles, as exemplary philosophers, authors of philosophical writings, ritual experts, teachers and students. Using the concept of instrumental agency enables us to appreciate more fully the ways in which these women also played significant roles in the formation and development of Platonist philosophical communities, as Heads, patrons and supporters of philosophical schools, and as empowering role models, especially in relation to ethics, specifically the cultivation of the virtues.

Due to space limitations, some of the roles of Platonist women have been outlined only briefly and merit further examination. The involvement of women in the production of philosophical works has been explored in greater depth: I argue that a wider range of women than usually acknowledged wrote philosophical works, and the lack of survival of their writings (or the lack of attribution of extant works to them) is affected by their social marginalisation and by residual prejudice relating to epistemic injustice in their own time and in subsequent traditions of textual transmission. Platonist women also played important instrumental roles in acting as significant catalysts for male-authored writings and the philosophical ideas examined therein. In both respects, women philosophers played a more significant role in textual production than often assumed. Additionally, many Platonist women were presented as philosopher-priestesses and played significant roles in the development and major trajectories of Platonism in this respect.

Women philosophers are often only mentioned briefly in male-authored works, making it difficult to ascertain their philosophical ideas, activities and contributions in detail or with certainty. The few women who receive a more detailed treatment, like Hypatia and Sosipatra, are often seen as anomalous (see, for example, Hawley 1994: 70–87). Yet these women's philosophical contributions are part of a much wider and fairly consistent picture of female activity within the Platonic tradition. The lack of focus on women in extant textual sources has contributed towards an underestimation of women's philosophical contributions. However, their significant roles as transmitters of philosophical knowledge and ideas, and of religious and ritual expertise, are evident, both in terms of intergenerational transmission from teacher to student and in relation to the longer-term transmission of exemplary role models. Faint traces of female-to-female philosophical transmission are also evident in our sources. This Element has additionally utilised relevant epigraphic and archaeological sources of evidence in attempting to illuminate the activities of Platonist women. It seems crucial to combine these different types of evidence in order to gain a fuller picture of women's philosophical roles. Overall, women played significant roles in the world of Plato, Middle Platonism and Neoplatonism; their contributions to the Platonic tradition and the history of Platonism should not be underestimated.

Abbreviations

Abbreviations of titles (including journal titles and epigraphic collections) are taken from Hornblower, S., Spawforth, A. and Edinow, E. (2012). *The Oxford Classical Dictionary*. 4th ed. Oxford: Oxford University Press. Exceptions are listed below.

Damascius
Phil. Hist.   *Philosophical History* (*Life of Isidore*)
Diogenes Laertius
D.L.   *Lives of Eminent Philosophers*
Iamblichus
DM   *De mysteriis*
Marinus
Proc.   *Proclus, Or On Happiness*
Porphyry
Marc.   *Letter to Marcella*
Inscriptions
I.Pergamon   *Die Inschriften von Pergamon,* ed. Frankel (1895).

References

Adamson, P. (2023). The Reception of Plato on Women: Proclus, Averroes, Marinella. In O'Reilly and Pellò 2023, 228–246.

Addey, C. (2014a). *Divination and Theurgy in Neoplatonism: Oracles of the Gods*. London: Routledge.

(2014b). The *Daimonion* of Socrates: *Daimones* and Divination in Neoplatonism. In D. A. Layne and H. Tarrant, eds. *The Neoplatonic Socrates*. Philadelphia: University of Pennsylvania Press, 51–72.

(2017). Plato's Women Readers. In H. Tarrant, D. A. Layne, D. Baltzly and F. Renaud, eds. *Brill's Companion to the Reception of Plato in Antiquity*. Leiden: Brill, 411–432.

(2018). Sosipatra: Prophetess, Philosopher and Theurgist: Reflections on Divination and Epistemology in Late Antiquity. In R. Evans, ed. *Prophets and Profits: Problems in Ancient Divination and Its Reception*. London: Routledge, 144–161.

(2022). Diotima, Sosipatra and Hypatia: Methodological Reflections on the Study of Female Philosophers in the Platonic Tradition. In Schultz and Wilberding 2022, 9–40.

(2024). The Reception of Diotima in Later Platonism: Clea, Sosipatra and Asclepigeneia. In Brill and McKeen 2024, 461–481.

Adler, A. (1935). *Suidas Lexicon*, vol. IV. Leipzig: Teubner.

Ahbel-Rappe, S. (2009). *Socrates: A Guide for the Perplexed*. London: Continuum.

Annas, J. (1976). Plato's Republic and Feminism. *Philosophy* 51, 307–321.

Arensen, K. (2023). Ancient Women Epicureans and Their Anti-Hedonist Critics. In O'Reilly and Pellò 2023, 77–95.

Armstrong, A. H. (1969–88). *Plotinus: Enneads. Porphyry: On the Life of Plotinus*. 2nd ed. 7 vols. Cambridge, MA: Harvard University Press.

Athanassiadi, P. (1999). *Damascius: The Philosophical History*. Athens: Apamea Cultural Association.

(2013). The Divine Man of Late Hellenism: A Sociable and Popular Figure. In M. Dzielska and K. Twardowska, eds. *Divine Men and Women in the History and Society of Late Hellenism*. Cracow: Jagiellonian University Press, 13–27.

Babbit, F. C. (1928–36). *Plutarch's Moralia*, vols. II–V. Cambridge, MA: Harvard University Press.

Bagnall, R. and Cribiore, R. (2015). *Women's Letters from Ancient Egypt, 300 BC – AD 800*. Ann Arbor: University of Michigan Press.

Baltes, M. (1993). Plato's School, the Academy. *Hermathena* 155, 5–26.

Balty, J. (1988). Apamea in Syria in the Second and Third Centuries A.D. *JRS* 78, 91–104.

Barnes, J. (2002). Ancient Philosophers. In Clark and Rajak 2002, 293–306.

Barrow, R. H. (1967). *Plutarch and His Times*. London: Chatto & Windus.

Bidez, J. (1913). *Vie de Porphyre, le philosophe neo-platonicien*. Ghent: Goethem.

(1960). *L'empereur Julien. Oeuvres complètes*, vol. 1.2, 2nd ed. Paris: Les Belles Lettres.

Bingham-Kolenkow, A. (2002). Persons of Power and Their Communities. In L. Ciraolo and J. Seidel, eds. *Magic and Divination in the Ancient World*. Leiden: Brill, 33–44.

Blair, E. D. (1996). Women: The Unrecognised Teachers of the Platonic Socrates. *Ancient Philosophy* 16, 333–350.

(2012). *Plato's Dialectic on Women: Equal Therefore Inferior*. London: Routledge.

Blok, J. (2001). Virtual Voices: Toward a Choreography of Women's Speech in Classical Athens. In A. Lardinois and L. McClure, eds. *Making Silence Speak: Women's Voices in Greek Literature and Society*. Princeton: Princeton University Press, 95–116.

Bonazzi, M. (2020). The End of the Academy. In P. Kalligas, C. Balla, E. Baziotopoulou-Valavaki and V. Karasmanis, eds. *Plato's Academy: Its Workings and Its History*. Cambridge: Cambridge University Press, 242–255.

Bowersock, G. W. (1965). Some Persons in Plutarch's *Moralia*. *CQ* 15(2), 267–270.

Boys-Stones, G. and Rowe, C. (2013). *The Circle of Socrates: Readings in the First-Generation Socratics*. Indianapolis: Hackett.

Brill, S. and McKeen, C. (eds.) (2024). *The Routledge Handbook of Women and Ancient Greek Philosophy*. London: Routledge.

Brisson, L. (2005). *Porphyrye Sentences. Études D'Introduction Text Grec et Traduction Francaise, Commentaire*. 2 vols. Paris: Vrin.

(2022). Marcella and Porphyry. In Schultz and Wilberding 2022, 64–78.

Brown, P. (1971). The Rise and Function of the Holy Man in Late Antiquity. *JRS* 61, 80–101.

Brüggemann, T., Kinzig, W. and Riedweg, C. (2016–17). *Kyrill von Alexandrien: Gegen Julian Buch 1–10 und Fragmente, Teil 1–2*. Berlin: De Gruyter.

Burkert, W. (1987). *Ancient Mystery Cults*. Cambridge, MA: Harvard University Press.

Burnet, J. (1967–68). *Platonis opera*, 2nd ed. 5 vols. Oxford: Clarendon.

Burrus, V. (2005). Is Macrina a Woman? Gregory of Nyssa's Dialogue on the Soul and Resurrection. In G. Ward, ed. *The Blackwell Companion to Postmodern Theology*. Oxford: Blackwell, 49–64.

Cameron, A. (1990). Isidore of Miletus and Hypatia: On the Editing of Mathematical Texts. *GRBS* 31(1), 103–127.

Cameron, A. and Long, J. (1993). *Barbarians and Politics at the Court of Arcadius*. Berkeley: University of California Press.

Christensen, A. R. (2023). Not Veiled in Silence: The Case for Macrina. In O'Reilly and Pellò 2023, 170–189.

Clark, E. (1998). The Lady Vanishes: Dilemmas of a Feminist Historian after the 'Linguistic Turn'. *Church History* 87(1), 1–31.

Clark, G. (1993). *Women in Late Antiquity: Pagan and Christian Lifestyles*. Oxford: Clarendon.

(2007). Do Try this at Home: The Domestic Philosopher in Late Antiquity. In H. Amirav and B. H. Romeny, eds. *From Rome to Constantinople: Studies in Honour of Averil Cameron*. Leuven: Peeters, 153–172.

Clark, G. and Rajak, T. (eds.) (2002). *Philosophy and Power in the Graeco-Roman World: Essays in Honour of Miriam Griffin*. Oxford: Oxford University Press.

Clarke, E., Dillon, J. and Hershbell, J. (2003). *Iamblichus: On the Mysteries*. Atlanta: SBL.

Clinton, K. (1974). *The Sacred Officials of the Eleusinian Mysteries*. Philadelphia: American Philosophical Society.

Cole, S. G. (1981). Could Greek Women Read and Write? *Women's Studies* 8(1–2), 129–155.

Connell, S. (2023). Women's Medical Knowledge in Antiquity: Beyond Midwifery. In O'Reilly and Pellò 2023, 57–76.

Connelly, J. B. (2007). *Portrait of a Priestess: Women and Ritual in Ancient Greece*. Princeton: Princeton University Press.

Cooper, K. (1996). *The Virgin and the Bride: Idealized Womanhood in Late Antiquity*. Cambridge, MA: Harvard University Press.

Corrigan, K. and Glazov-Corrigan, E. (2004). *Plato's Dialectic at Play: Argument, Structure and Myth in the Symposium*. University Park: Pennsylvania State University Press.

Corsten, T. (2010). *Lexicon of Greek Personal Names: Volume V. Coastal Asia Minor: Pontos to Ionia*. Oxford: Clarendon.

Cox, P. (1983). *Biography in Late Antiquity: A Quest for the Holy Man*. Berkeley: University of California.

D'Angour, A. (2019). *Socrates in Love: The Making of a Philosopher*. London: Bloomsbury.

Deakin, M. A. B. (1994). Hypatia and Her Mathematics. *American Mathematical Monthly* 101(3), 234–243.

Dean-Jones, L. (1995). Menexenus – Son of Socrates. *CQ* 45(1), 51–57.

Denzey Lewis, N. (2014). Living Images of the Divine: Female Theurgists in Late Antiquity. In K. B. Stratton and D. S. Kalleres, eds. *Daughters of Hecate: Women and Magic in the Ancient World*. Oxford: Oxford University Press, 274–297.

Deslauriers, M. (2012). Women, Education and Philosophy. In S. L. James and S. Dillon, eds. *A Companion to Women in the Ancient World*. Oxford: Blackwell, 343–353.

Diduch, P. J. and Harding, M. P. (eds.) (2018). *Socrates in the Cave: On the Philosopher's Motive in Plato*. Cham: Palgrave Macmillan.

Dillon, J. (1996). *The Middle Platonists. 80 BC to AD 220*. 2nd ed. Ithaca: Cornell University Press.

  (2003). *The Heirs of Plato: A Study of the Old Academy (347–274 BC)*. Oxford: Clarendon.

  (2004). Philosophy as a Profession in Late Antiquity. In S. Swain and M. Edwards, eds. *Approaching Late Antiquity: The Transformation from Early to Late Empire*. Oxford: Oxford University Press, 401–418.

  (2022). Theodorus of Asine on the Equality of the Sexes: Traces of a Rhetorical Trope in the Fourth Century CE. In Schultz and Wilberding 2022, 94–103.

Dillon, J. and Hershbell, J. (eds.) (1991). *Iamblichus: On the Pythagorean Way of Life (De Vita Pythagorica)*. Atlanta: Scholars Press.

Dillon, J. and Polleichtner, W. (eds.) (2009). *Iamblichus of Chalcis: The Letters*. Atlanta: SBL.

Dillon, M. (2013). Engendering the Scroll: Girls' and Women's Literacy in Classical Greece. In J. E. Grubbs and T. Parkin, eds. *The Oxford Handbook of Childhood and Education in the Classical World*. Oxford: Oxford University Press, 396–417.

Dittenberger, G. (1897). *Inscriptiones Graecae* IX, I. Berlin: Reimer.

Dixon, S. (2001). *Reading Roman Women*. London: Duckworth.

Donnay, G. (1984). Instrument divinatoire d'epoque romaine. In J. Balthy, ed. *Apamée de Syrie. Bilan des recherches archelogiques 1973=1979. Actes du collque 1980*. Brussels: Centre belge de recherches archéologiques à Apamée de Syrie, 203–212.

Dorandi, T. (1989). Assiotea e Lastenia: due donne all' Academia. *Atti e memorie dell' Accademia Toscana di scienze e lettere La Colombaria* 54, 51–66.

(2013). *Diogenes Laertius: Lives of Eminent Philosophers*. Cambridge: Cambridge University Press.

Dover, K. J. (1965). The Date of Plato's *Symposium*. *Phronesis* 10(1), 2–20.

(1966). Aristophanes' Speech in Plato's *Symposium*. *JHS* 86, 41–50.

Dzielska, M. (1995). *Hypatia of Alexandria*. Trans. F. Lyra. Cambridge, MA: Harvard University Press.

Edwards, M. (2000). *Neoplatonic Saints: The Lives of Plotinus and Proclus by Their Students*. Liverpool: Liverpool University Press.

Eule, J. C. (2001). *Hellenistische Bürgerinnen aus Kleinasien: Weibliche Gewandstatuen in ihrem antiken Kontext*. Istanbul: TASK.

Evans, N. (2006). Diotima and Demeter as Mystagogues in Plato's *Symposium*. *Hypatia* 21(2), 1–27.

Finamore, J. (2012). Iamblichus on the Grades of Virtue. In E. Afonasin, J. Dillon and J. Finamore, eds. *Iamblichus and the Foundations of Platonism*. Leiden: Brill, 113–132.

Fowden, G. (1982). The Pagan Holy Man in Late Antique Society. *JHS* 102, 33–59.

Frank, K., Gilles, G., Plastow, C. and Webb, L. (2024). *Female Agency in the Ancient Mediterranean*. Liverpool: Liverpool University Press.

Frankel, M. (1895). *Die Inschriften von Pergamon*, Band VIII.2: *Romische Zeit*. Berlin: Reimer.

Fricker, M. (2007). *Epistemic Injustice: Power and the Ethics of Knowing*. Oxford: Oxford University Press.

Gaiser, K. (1988). *Philodems Academica: Die Beruchte über Platon und die Alte Akademie in zwei herkulanensischen Papyri*. Stuttgart: Frommann Holzboog.

Garside Allen, C. (1975). Plato on Women. *Feminist Studies* 2, 131–138.

Garzys, A. (2000). *Synésios de Cyrène. Tome* II: *Correspondance: Lettres* I–LXIII. Paris: Les Belles Lettres.

Geertz, S. (2020). 'A Mere Geometer'? Hypatia in the Context of Alexandrian Neoplatonism. In LaValle Norman and Petkas 2020, 133–150.

Giangrande, J. (1956). *Eunapii vitae sophistarum*. Rome: Polygraphica.

Gilhuly, K. (2008). *The Feminine Matrix of Sex and Gender in Classical Athens*. Cambridge: Cambridge University Press.

Gordon, R. (2002). Another View of the Pergamon Divination Kit. *JRA* 15, 188–198.

Hadot, P. (1993). *Plotinus or the Simplicity of Vision*. Trans. M. Chase. Chicago: University of Chicago Press.

(1995). *Philosophy as a Way of Life: Spiritual Exercises from Socrates to Foucault*. Trans. M. Chase. Malden: Blackwell.

(2002). *What Is Ancient Philosophy?* Cambridge, MA: Harvard University Press.

Halperin, D. M. (1990). Why Is Diotima a Woman? Platonic Erōs and the Configuration of Gender. In D. M. Halperin, J. J. Winkler and F. I. Zeitlin, eds. *Before Sexuality: The Construction of Erotic Experience in the Ancient Greek World*. Princeton: Princeton University Press, 257–308.

Hawley, R. (1994). The Problem of Women Philosophers in Ancient Greece. In L. J. Archer, S. Fischler and M. Wyke, eds. *Women in Ancient Societies: An Illusion of the Night*. London: Macmillan, 70–87.

(1999). Practicing What You Preach: Plutarch's Sources and Treatment. In Pomeroy 1999, 116–127.

Hendrickson, G. L. and Hubbell, H. M. (1939). *Cicero. Brutus. Orator.* Cambridge, MA: Harvard University Press.

Henry, M. M. (1995). *Prisoner of History: Aspasia of Miletus and Her Biographical Tradition*. Oxford: Oxford University Press.

Hutton, S. (2015). Blue-Eyed Philosophers Born on Wednesdays: An Essay on Women and the History of Philosophy. *Monist* 98, 7–20.

Jackson, K. (2012). 'She Who Changes' (*Amibousa*): A Re-examination of the Triangular Table from Pergamon. *JRA* 25, 455–474.

Jannoray, J. (1946). Inscriptions delphiques d'époque tardive: Inscriptions de Lébadée. *BCH* 70, 247–262.

Johnston, S. I. (2012). Sosipatra and the Theurgic Life: Eunapius *Vitae Sophistorum* 6.6.5–6.9.24. In J. Rüpke and W. Spickermann, eds. *Reflections on Religious Individuality: Greco-Roman and Judaeo-Christian Texts and Practices*. Berlin: De Gruyter, 99–117.

Jones, C. P. (1966). Towards a Chronology of Plutarch's Works. *JRS* 56(1–2), 61–74.

Kalligas, P., Balla, C., Baziotopoulou-Valavaki, E. and Karasmanis, V. (eds.) (2020). *Plato's Academy: Its Workings and Its History*. Cambridge: Cambridge University Press.

Kapetanopoulos, E. A. (1966). Klea and Leontis: Two Ladies from Delphi. *BCH* 90(1), 119–130.

Keime, C. (2016). The Role of Diotima in the *Symposium*: The Dialogue and Its Double. In G. Cornelli, ed. *Plato's Styles and Characters: Between Literature and Philosophy*. Berlin: De Gruyter, 379–395.

Keller, M. (2002). *The Hammer and the Flute: Women, Power and Spirit Possession*. Baltimore: John Hopkins University Press.

Kranz, W. (1926). Diotima von Mantinea. *Hermes* 61 (II.4), 437–447.

Lamb, W. R. M. (1924). *Plato. Laches. Protagoras. Meno. Euthydemus*. Cambridge, MA: Harvard University Press.

Langlands, R. (2004). A Woman's Influence on a Roman Text: Marcia and Seneca. In McHardy and Marshall 2004, 115–126.

Lavalle Norman, D. (2022). *Early Christian Women*. Cambridge Elements: Women in the History of Philosophy. Cambridge: Cambridge University Press.

Lavalle Norman, D. and Petkas, A. (eds.) (2020). *Hypatia of Alexandria: Her Context and Legacy*. Tübingen: Mohr Siebeck.

Layne, D. (2024). Divine Names and the Mystery of Diotima. In Brill and MacKeen 2024, 247–283.

(2026). The Mysterious Gift of Platonic Mothers. A Spectral Solution to a Postmodern Dilemma. In G. Shaw and C. Stang, eds. *Platonism as a Living Tradition*. Cambridge, MA: Harvard University Press.

Levin, S. (1975). Diotima's Visit and Service to Athens. *Grazer Beiträge* 4, 223–240.

Long, A. A. (2018). Introduction. In J. Miller, ed. *Diogenes Laertius: Lives of the Eminent Philosophers*. Oxford: Oxford University Press, xv–xxiv.

Loraux, N. (1986). *The Invention of Athens: The Funeral Oration in the Classical City*. Cambridge, MA: Harvard University Press.

Marx, H. (2021). *Sosipatra of Pergamum: Philosopher and Oracle*. Oxford: Oxford University Press.

Mastrocinque, A. (2002). The Divinatory Kit from Pergamon and Greek Magic in Late Antiquity. *JRA* 15, 173–187.

McCoy, M. B. (2024). Socratic Midwifery. In Brill and MacKeen 2024, 253–266.

McHardy, F. and Marshall, E. (eds.) (2004). *Women's Influence on Classical Civilisation*. Abingdon: Routledge.

McLoughlin, G. (2004). The Logistics of Gender from Classical Philosophy. In McHardy and Marshall 2004, 7–25.

Mendelssohn, I. (1887). *Zosimus: New History*. Leipzig: Teubner.

Merchant, E. C. (1971). *Xenophontis opera omnia*, vol. 2. Oxford: Clarendon.

Migne, J. P. (1864). *Synesius Cyrenensis Opera Omnia*. PG 66. Paris: Imprimerie Catholique.

Miller, J. and Mensch, P. (2018). *Diogenes Laertius: Lives of the Eminent Philosophers*. Oxford: Oxford University Press.

Möbius, H. (1934). Diotima. *Jahrbuch des Deutschen Archäologischen Instituts* 49, 45–60.

Nachstädt, W. (1935 [1971]). *Plutarchi moralia*, vol. 2.1. Leipzig: Teubner.
Nails, D. (2002). *The People of Plato: A Prosopography of Plato and Other Socratics*. Indianapolis: Hackett.
  (2015). Bad Luck to Take a Woman Aboard. In H. Tarrant and D. Nails, eds. *Second Sailing: Alternative Perspectives on Plato*. Helsinki: Societas Scientarium Fennica, 73–90.
Nehamas, A. and Woodruff, P. (1989). *Plato, Symposium*. Indianapolis: Hackett.
Neugebauer, O. (1975). *A History of Ancient Mathematical Astronomy*. Berlin: Springer.
Nightingale, A. (2021). *Philosophy and Religion in Plato's Dialogues*. Cambridge: Cambridge University Press.
Nye, A. (2015). *Socrates and Diotima: Sexuality, Religion and the Nature of Divinity*. Cham: Palgrave Macmillan.
O'Brien Wicker, K. (ed.) (1987). *Porphyry the Philosopher: To Marcella*. Atlanta: Scholars Press.
Okin, S. M. (1977). Philosopher Queens and Private Wives: Plato on Women and the Family. *Philosophy and Public Affairs* 6(4), 345–369.
O'Meara, D. (2003). *Platonopolis: Platonic Political Philosophy in Late Antiquity*. Oxford: Clarendon.
O'Reilly, R. and Pellò, C. (eds.) (2023). *Ancient Women Philosophers: Recovered Ideas and New Perspectives*. Cambridge: Cambridge University Press.
Pappas, N. and Zelcer, M. (2015). *Politics and Philosophy in Plato's Menexenus: Education and Rhetoric, Myth and History*. London: Routledge.
Pellò, C. (2022). *Pythagorean Women*. Cambridge Elements: Women in the History of Philosophy. Cambridge: Cambridge University Press.
Penella, R. J. (1990). *Greek Philosophers and Sophists in the Fourth Century A. D.: Studies in Eunapius of Sardis*. Leeds: Cairns.
Plant, I. M. (2004). *Women Writers of Ancient Greece and Rome: An Anthology*. Norman: University of Oklahoma.
Pomeroy, S. B. (1974). Feminism in Book V of Plato's *Republic*. *Apeiron* 8, 33–35.
  (ed.) (1999). *Plutarch's Advice to the Bride and Groom and a Consolation to His Wife*. Oxford: Oxford University Press.
Puech, B. (1992). Prosopographie des amis de Plutarque. *ANRW* II.33.6, 4831–4893.
Reeve, C. D. C. (2001). *Women in the Academy: Dialogues on Themes from Plato's Republic*. Indianapolis: Hackett.
Riedwig, C. (2002). *Pythagoras: His Life, Teaching, and Influence*. Ithaca: Cornell University Press.

Riginos, A. S. (1976). *Platonica: The Anecdotes Concerning the Life and Writings of Plato*. Leiden: Brill.

Rist, J. M. (1965). Hypatia. *Phoenix* 19(3), 214–225.

Robinson, D. M. and Blegen, E. P. (1935). Archaeological News and Discussions. *AJArch* 39(3), 378–411.

Robitzsch, J. M. (2017). On Aspasia in Plato's *Menexenus*. *Phoenix* 71(3/4), 288–300.

Rome, A. (ed.) (1943). *Commentaires de Pappus et de Theon d'Alexandria sur l'Algameste*, vol. 3. Rome: Biblioteca apostolica Vaticana.

Rosenstock, B. (1994). Socrates as Revenant: A Reading of the *Menexenus*. *Phoenix* 48(4), 331–347.

Roskam, G. (2021). *Plutarch*. Cambridge: Cambridge University Press.

Roussel, P. (1923). *Supplementum Epigraphicum Graecum*. Leiden: Sijthoff.

Russell, D. A. (1973). *Plutarch*. London: Duckworth.

Saffrey, H. D. (2001). *Marinus: Proclus ou sur le bonheur*. Paris: Les Belles Lettres.

Sandbach, F. H. (1969). *Plutarch's Moralia: Fragments*, vol. XV. Cambridge, MA: Harvard University Press.

Santoro, F. (2016). Orphic Aristophanes at Plato's Symposium. In G. Cornelli, ed. *Plato's Styles and Characters: Between Literature and Philosophy*. Berlin: De Gruyter, 211–226.

Saxonhouse, A. W. (1984). Eros and the Female in Greek Political Thought: An Interpretation of Plato's *Symposium*. *Political Theory* 12(1), 5–27.

Schultz, J. (2022). Damascius on the Virtue of Women and Their Relation to Men. In Schultz and Wilberding 2022, 122–143.

(2023). Women Philosophers and Ideals of Being a Woman in Neoplatonic Schools of Late Antiquity: The Examples of Sosipatra of Ephesus and Hypatia of Alexandria. In O'Reilly and Pellò 2023, 190–207.

Schultz, J. and Wilberding, J. (eds.) (2022). *Women and the Female in Neoplatonism*. Leiden: Brill.

Sesiano, J. (1982). *Books IV to VII of Diophantus' Arithemetica*. New York: Springer.

Sheffield, F. C. C. (2006). *Plato's Symposium: The Ethics of Desire*. Oxford: Oxford University Press.

(2023). Beyond Gender: The Voice of Diotima. In O'Reilly and Pellò 2023, 21–37.

Sieveking, W. (1972). *Plutarchi moralia*, vol. 3. 2nd ed. Leipzig: Teubner.

Slaveva-Griffin, S. (2016). Asclepian Souls in Late Antiquity. *Numen* 63(2–3), 167–195.

Slings, S. R. (2003). *Platonis Rempublicam*. Oxford: Oxford University Press.

Snyder, J. M. (1989). *The Woman and the Lyre: Women Writers in Classical Greece and Rome*. Bristol: Bristol Classical.

Stadter, P. A. (1999). *Philosophos kai Philandros*: Plutarch's View of Women in the *Moralia* and *Lives*. In Pomeroy 1999, 173–182.

Tanaseanu-Döbler, I. (2013). Sosipatra – Role Models for Pagan 'Divine' Women in Late Antiquity. In M. Dzielska and K. Twardowska, eds. *Divine Men and Women in the History and Society of Late Hellenism*. Krakow: Jagiellonian University Press, 123–147.

Tarrant, H., Layne, D. A., Baltzly, D. and Renaud, F. (eds.) (2017). *Brill's Companion to the Reception of Plato in Antiquity*. Leiden: Brill, 1–7.

Thomas, R. (1989). *Oral Tradition and Written Record in Classical Athens*. Cambridge: Cambridge University Press.

Toomer, G. J. (1984). Tr. *Ptolemy. Algamest*. London: Duckworth.

Twomey, R. (2023). Pythagorean Women and the Domestic as a Philosophical Topic. In O'Reilly and Pellò 2023, 134–151.

Tyldesley, J. (1994). *Daughters of Isis: Women of Ancient Egypt*. London: Penguin.

Von Willamowitz-Moellendorff, U. (1995). Plutarch as Biographer. In B. Scardigli, ed. *Essays on Plutarch's Lives*. Oxford: Clarendon, 47–74.

Watts, E. (2005). Orality and Communal Identity in Eunapius'. *Lives of the Sophists and Philosophers. Byzantion* 75, 334–361.

(2007). Creating the Academy: Historical Discourse and the Shape of Community in the Old Academy. *JHS* 127, 106–122.

(2017). *Hypatia: The Life and Legend of an Ancient Philosopher*. Oxford: Oxford University Press.

Wehrli, F. (1967). *Die Schule des Aristoteles vol. 1, Dikaiarchos*, 2nd ed. Stuttgart: Schwabe.

Whittaker, H. (2001). The Purpose of Porphyry's *Letter to Marcella*. *Symbolae Osloenses* 76, 150–168.

Wilberding, J. (2022). Women in Plotinus. In Schultz and Wilberding 2022, 43–63.

Wright, W. C. (1913–23). *The Works of the Emperor Julian*, vol. II–III. Cambridge, MA: Harvard University Press.

(1921). *Philostratus. Lives of the Sophists. Eunapius. Lives of Philosophers*. Cambridge, MA: Harvard University Press.

Wünsch, R. (1905). *Antikes Zaubergerift aux Pergamon*. Berlin: Georg Reimer.

Zhmud, L. (2012). *Pythagoras and the Early Pythagoreans*. Oxford: Oxford University Press.

Ziegler, K. (1964). *Plutarchi vitae parallelae*, vol. 1.2. Leipzig: Teubner.

Acknowledgements

I wish to thank Jacqueline Broad, the series editor, for her support and patience. Many thanks to audiences in Cambridge, Cork and Dublin for their comments on presentations of this material. I thank the National Archaeological Museum, Athens, and the Hellenic Ministry of Culture (Hellenic Organization of Cultural Resources Department) and the Antikensammlung Staatliche Museen zu Berlin for permission to reprint Figures 1 and 2 respectively. Many thanks to Sara Ahbel-Rappe, John Finamore, Michael Griffin, Dawn LaValle Norman, Danielle Layne, Máirín MacCarron, Caterina Pellò, Mark Usher, Etain Addey, Tim Addey, and the anonymous reviewers for helpful comments on earlier drafts. I dedicate this work to my mother, Averil Addey.

Cambridge Elements =

Women in the History of Philosophy

Jacqueline Broad
Monash University

Jacqueline Broad is Professor of Philosophy at Monash University, Australia. Her area of expertise is early modern philosophy, with a special focus on seventeenth and eighteenth-century women philosophers. She is the author of *Women Philosophers of the Seventeenth Century* (Cambridge University Press, 2002), *A History of Women's Political Thought in Europe, 1400–1700* (with Karen Green; Cambridge University Press, 2009), and *The Philosophy of Mary Astell: An Early Modern Theory of Virtue* (Oxford University Press, 2015).

Advisory Board
Dirk Baltzly, *University of Tasmania*
Sandrine Bergès, *Bilkent University*
Marguerite Deslauriers, *McGill University*
Karen Green, *University of Melbourne*
Lisa Shapiro, *McGill University*
Emily Thomas, *Durham University*

About the Series
In this Cambridge Elements series, distinguished authors provide concise and structured introductions to a comprehensive range of prominent and lesser-known figures in the history of women's philosophical endeavour, from ancient times to the present day.

Cambridge Elements

Women in the History of Philosophy

Elements in the Series

Mary Shepherd
Antonia LoLordo

Mary Wollstonecraft
Martina Reuter

Susan Stebbing
Frederique Janssen-Lauret

Harriet Taylor Mill
Helen McCabe

Victoria Welby
Emily Thomas

Nísia Floresta
Nastassja Pugliese

Catharine Trotter Cockburn
Ruth Boeker

Lucrezia Marinella
Marguerite Deslauriers

Amalia Holst
Andrew Cooper

Iris Murdoch
Bridget Clarke

E. E. Constance Jones
Gary Ostertag

Platonist Women
Crystal Addey

A full series listing is available at: www.cambridge.org/EWHP

For EU product safety concerns, contact us at Calle de José Abascal, 56–1°, 28003 Madrid, Spain or eugpsr@cambridge.org.

www.ingramcontent.com/pod-product-compliance
Lightning Source LLC
LaVergne TN
LVHW011850060526
838200LV00054B/4269